T0311687

Cambridge Elements ≡

Elements in Forensic Linguistics
edited by
Tim Grant
Aston University
Tammy Gales
Hofstra University

A THEORY OF LINGUISTIC INDIVIDUALITY FOR AUTHORSHIP ANALYSIS

Andrea Nini
University of Manchester

CAMBRIDGE
UNIVERSITY PRESS

Shaftesbury Road, Cambridge CB2 8EA, United Kingdom

One Liberty Plaza, 20th Floor, New York, NY 10006, USA

477 Williamstown Road, Port Melbourne, VIC 3207, Australia

314–321, 3rd Floor, Plot 3, Splendor Forum, Jasola District Centre, New Delhi – 110025, India

103 Penang Road, #05–06/07, Visioncrest Commercial, Singapore 238467

Cambridge University Press is part of Cambridge University Press & Assessment, a department of the University of Cambridge.

We share the University's mission to contribute to society through the pursuit of education, learning and research at the highest international levels of excellence.

www.cambridge.org
Information on this title: www.cambridge.org/9781108971386

DOI: 10.1017/9781108974851

First published 2023

A catalogue record for this publication is available from the British Library.

ISBN 978-1-108-97138-6 Paperback
ISSN 2634-7334 (online)
ISSN 2634-7326 (print)

Additional resources for this publication at www.cambridge.org/nini.

A Theory of Linguistic Individuality for Authorship Analysis

Elements in Forensic Linguistics

DOI: 10.1017/9781108974851
First published online: May 2023

Andrea Nini
University of Manchester
Author for correspondence: Andrea Nini, andrea.nini@manchester.ac.uk

Abstract: Authorship analysis is the process of determining who produced a questioned text by language analysis. Although there has been significant success in the performance of computational methods to solve this problem in recent years, these are often methods that are not amenable to interpretation. Authorship analysis is to all effects an area of computer science with very little linguistics or cognitive science. This Element introduces a *Theory of Linguistic Individuality* that, starting from basic notions of cognitive linguistics, establishes a formal framework for the mathematical modelling of language processing that is then applied to three computational experiments, including using the likelihood ratio framework. The results propose new avenues of research and a change of perspective in the way authorship analysis is currently carried out. This Element is also available as Open Access on Cambridge Core.

Keywords: computational linguistics, idiolect, cognitive linguistics, forensic science, authorship analysis

ISBNs: 9781108971386 (PB), 9781108974851 (OC)
ISSNs: 2634-7334 (online), 2634-7326 (print)

Contents

Series Preface

The Elements in Forensic Linguistics series from Cambridge University Press publishes across four main topic areas: (1) investigative and forensic text analysis; (2) the study of spoken linguistic practices in legal contexts; (3) the linguistic analysis of written legal texts; (4) explorations of the origins, development, and scope of the field in various countries and regions. Situated in the first of these areas, *A Theory of Linguistic Individuality for Authorship Analysis* by Andrea Nini significantly advances our understanding of the linguistic individual.

One of the basic premises underlying studies of questioned authorship is that every individual has their own unique way of speaking and writing – an idiolect. Previous scholars have emphasised the importance of co-selection, or the distinct combination of choices made by an individual, in the process of creating an individual style. Yet, to date, we do not have an adequate theory that explains how or why such unique linguistic individuality exists.

As an established scholar and practitioner in the area of authorship identification, Nini's work has focused on quantitative analyses of literary and linguistic style, linguistic profiling, and authorship analysis. In this Element, he draws on this expertise and combines theories and research traditions from linguistics, computer science, and mathematics in order to lay the foundation for just such a theory. The results from his three empirical studies provide promising support for the theory, demonstrate how likelihood ratio frameworks suitable for legal conclusions can be implemented, and suggest valuable avenues for further research.

With our second Element in the series to raise challenging questions related to disputed authorship (see also Tim Grant's Element, *The Idea of Progress in Forensic Authorship Analysis*), we encourage researchers from all related fields to continue contributing to the theoretical and practical development of this important field.

Tammy Gales
Series Editor

1 Introduction

The task of determining the likelihood that a person produced a text based on the language goes by various names, such as *authorship analysis*, *authorship attribution*, or *authorship identification*. Even though these terms have been used as synonyms in previous work, the present Element adopts the term *comparative authorship analysis* to indicate this task, or just *authorship analysis* for brevity, following Grant's (2022) taxonomy. The term *authorship analysis* is therefore used in this work to encompass all those tasks that involve the study of texts of questioned authorship when at least one suspect author is present, whether this is a small or closed set of suspects or an open one, such as in *authorship verification* (Koppel and Schler, 2004; Koppel and Winter, 2014).

In principle, because it uses information about language usage, authorship analysis should be a fundamentally *linguistic* task, in that it is based on scientific principles and methods of linguistics. At the present moment, however, this is not really the case because the most significant advances in the field have been made mostly by computer scientists. This disassociation between authorship analysis and linguistics is not acceptable because the ideal goal would be to have a method that is both efficient and reliable and scientifically realistic. The purpose of this Element is precisely to put forward a Theory of Linguistic Individuality that bridges the gap between our scientific understanding of language processing and the computational methods now common in authorship analysis. Before moving to the theory itself, this section introduces the reader to the most important advances in authorship analysis first and then to the fundamental concepts borrowed from linguistics before building the theory in Section 2.

1.1 Authorship Analysis

The analysis of language to determine who authored a text is a practice that has been around for millennia, most prominently in literary studies, where scholars of particular author styles tended to rely on their own expert judgement (Coulthard *et al.*, 2017). Work on the quantification of stylistic features began in the nineteenth century, leading to the emergence of the new field of *stylometry*. The initial quest of stylometry was to find *author-invariant* features that would remain constant for each single author over time and genre. Despite thousands of authorship analysis features being tested, however, so far no such feature has been found.

The most important breakthrough in stylometry is without any doubt Mosteller and Wallace's (1963) analysis of the Federalist Papers. Approaching a text from the perspective of a statistician, Mosteller and Wallace focused on the frequencies of *function words*, such as articles, prepositions, or pronouns. Their reason for only considering the 'filler words of the language' was their obliviousness to topic and because 'they provide fairly stable rates' (Mosteller and Wallace, 1963, p. 275). This insight survived the test of time and to this day the analysis of word frequencies and especially of the frequency of function words is still among the most successful ways of carrying out authorship analysis (Grieve, 2007; Stamatatos, 2009; Argamon, 2018). The only other widely successful feature in modern stylometry has been the frequency of *n-grams*: sequences of length *n* collected using a moving window, in particular the frequency of character n-grams with small *n* (2 to 4) (Stamatatos, 2013). This type of character n-gram actually ends up also capturing a lot of the information carried by function words and therefore some of its usefulness can still be reconducted to the same fundamental criteria introduced by Mosteller and Wallace (1963).

Although there is mostly agreement on the best features for authorship analysis, there is less consensus on how to use them. The basic distinction in the field is between *similarity-based* and *machine learning* approaches (Stamatatos, 2009; Koppel *et al.*, 2013). In the first approach type, a similarity score is calculated for each text (or for an author's profile, which is a combination of the author's texts) and then this score is used to rank the candidate authors in terms of similarity to the questioned text, with the most similar being declared the correct author. In the second approach type, each text of known authorship is treated independently and a statistical model of how the candidate authors write is extracted. This model, generated using tools such as Principal Component Analysis, cluster analysis, multidimensional scaling, discriminant analysis, Support Vector Machine, or deep learning algorithms, is then used to determine who wrote the questioned text (Juola, 2008; Stamatatos, 2009; Argamon, 2018; Kestemont *et al.*, 2020). In the most specific case of authorship verification, that is when there is only one candidate author, the *General Impostors* algorithm has been found to be very effective. This algorithm is based on the idea of creating a line-up of fake candidates before applying a similarity-based analysis. If the similarity is greater for the candidate than for the impostors over multiple random tests with random sets of impostors and features, then the questioned text is assigned to the candidate author (Seidman, 2013; Koppel and Winter, 2014; Kestemont *et al.*, 2016).

1.2 Burrow's Delta

In order to execute the General Impostors method or any similarity-based analysis, a score that expresses a measure of similarity or distance must be used. There are many ways of measuring similarity/distance but decades of research in stylometry have now firmly demonstrated that the most effective of them for authorship analysis is *Delta* (Burrows, 2002).

The original Delta introduced by Burrows (2002) is calculated starting from the relative frequencies, f, of the top N most frequent words in the corpus considered, a relative frequency being the number of times the word is found in the text divided by the total number of word tokens in the text. For each of these most frequent words, firstly a *z-score* is calculated, which is a measure of deviation from the mean calculated by subtracting the mean, μ, of the relative frequency of the word considered from its relative frequency, and dividing this quantity by the standard deviation, σ. Once this is done for all the words considered, the Delta distance between texts A and B, $\Delta_{(A,B)}$, is calculated by taking the average of the absolute differences across all z-scores:

$$\Delta_{(A,B)} = \frac{1}{N}\sum_{i=1}^{N}|z_i(A) - z_i(B)|.$$

For example, suppose we have only two words, *the* and *of*, so $N = 2$, and the table of counts for these two features for two texts A and B is Table 1.

In this example, the relative frequencies would be (multiplied by 100 to make them easier to read):

$$f_{the}(A) = \tfrac{56}{800} * 100 = 7 \text{ and } f_{the}(B) = \tfrac{27}{900} * 100 = 3$$
$$f_{of}(A) = \tfrac{32}{800} * 100 = 4 \text{ and } f_{of}(B) = \tfrac{90}{900} * 100 = 10.$$

Let's imagine that we have more texts and that we calculate the mean and standard deviations for the relative frequencies of *the* and *of*, which are as follows:

$$\mu_{the} = 2 \quad \text{and} \quad \mu_{of} = 2$$
$$\sigma_{the} = 1 \quad \text{and} \quad \sigma_{of} = 2.$$

At this point it is possible to transform the relative frequencies, f_i, into z-scores, z_i, which indicate how different each relative frequency is from the mean.

With the z-scores it is now possible to plug in the values in the Delta formula to calculate the Delta distance between these two texts:

$$
\begin{aligned}
\Delta_{(A,B)} &= \frac{1}{2}\sum_{i=1}^{2}|z_i(A) - z_i(B)| = \\
&= \frac{|z_{the}(A) - z_{the}(B)| + |z_{of}(A) - z_{of}(B)|}{2} = \\
&= \frac{|5 - 1| + |1 - 4|}{2} = \frac{4 + 3}{2} = 3.5
\end{aligned}
$$

To put this in non-mathematical terms, by quantifying how much each author deviates from the norm, Delta is a measure of how much two texts are similar to each other in respect to how much they differ from a norm.

Table 1 Simple example of word counts for two toy texts and two function words.

	the	*of*	Total number of words
Text A	56	32	800
Text B	27	90	900

This simple formula has solidly passed the test of time and is one of the greatest achievements in authorship analysis (e.g. Hoover, 2004; Juola, 2012; Eder, 2015; Evert *et al.*, 2015, 2017). Repeated experiments have demonstrated that if enough register-compatible data for each author is collected then the values of Delta will be relatively small for texts that are written by the same author and relatively large for texts written by different authors. Delta can be used to attribute a text or to narrow down a large list of candidates because candidate authors can be ranked from more distant to less distant from a questioned text.

Even in the age of neural networks and deep learning algorithms, simple variations of this method are still extremely reliable. For example, Halvani *et al.* (2020) used a method that is very similar to Delta and that still performed very well compared to artificial intelligence methods. Similarly, Narayanan *et al.* (2012) and Pokhriyal *et al.* (2017) show how methods based on distances similar to Delta are optimal even in scenarios including thousands of authors and relatively short texts. In sum, Delta is a simple and largely transparent technique that has been found to work in various independent replications. However, despite this success, relatively little has been done to untangle the inner mechanisms responsible for this performance.

1.2.1 The Key Profiles Hypothesis

The first significant advance in the mathematical understanding of Delta is Argamon's (2008) geometric reinterpretation. Let's now imagine Table 2 not as a table of z-scored frequencies but as a Cartesian bidimensional space where each word is a dimension, like in Figure 1.

In this space, we can represent the two texts A and B as two points with their coordinates being the z-scores of the words *the* and *of*, thus:

$$A = \begin{bmatrix} 1 \\ 5 \end{bmatrix}, \quad B = \begin{bmatrix} 4 \\ 1 \end{bmatrix},$$

where the top row is for *of* and the bottom row is for *the*. These mathematical objects are called *vectors* and they can be represented as arrows that start from the origin of the space and reach the points. In this two-dimensional space, Delta is simply the *Manhattan distance* between these two points:

$$d_M = \sum_{i=1}^{N} |A_i - B_i|. \tag{1}$$

The Manhattan distance is so called because it is the distance between two points if we imagine driving or walking in a city like Manhattan, where it would be impossible to reach a destination by taking the quickest trajectory, a straight

Table 2 Relative frequencies from Table 1 transformed into z-scores.

	$z_{the} = \frac{f_{the} - \mu_{the}}{\sigma_{the}}$	$z_{of} = \frac{f_{of} - \mu_{of}}{\sigma_{of}}$
Text A	5	1
Text B	1	4

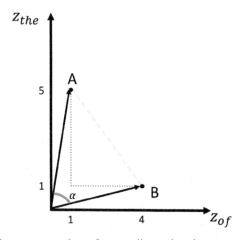

Figure 1 Simple representation of a two-dimensional vector space containing two texts, *A* and *B*.

line. This straight distance, which is called the *Euclidean distance*, is represented in Figure 1 as the dashed line connecting *A* and *B*. The Manhattan distance between *A* and *B* is instead the L-shaped path between *A* and *B* following the dotted line. Using the formula above, the calculation of the Manhattan distance in this case would be $|1 - 4| + |5 - 1| = 3 + 4 = 7$, which is the same result obtained above for Delta, just without the division by 2. Because *N* is a constant number for any pair of texts involved, dividing by it is an unnecessary step and therefore the Manhattan distance between these two vectors is the same as Delta. When calculating Delta, instead of two dimensions there are hundreds or thousands of words and, thus, hundreds or thousands of dimensions but the formula remains the same. Argamon's (2008) insight is useful and increases our mathematical understanding of Delta but it is more like a rephrasing than an explanation. We still do not know why or how the Manhattan distance between two vectors of frequencies works so well to identify authors.

Further explanatory advancements were made a few years later by Evert *et al.* (2015, 2017). As a first step, Evert *et al.* (2017) compared various versions of

Delta, such as traditional Delta (with the Manhattan distance), Quadratic Delta (with the Euclidean distance), and Cosine Delta (with the Cosine distance) using the *refcor* corpus, a multilingual corpus of novels collected from Project Gutenberg.[1] Looking back at Figure 1, Quadratic Delta would be the straight line between the two points, while Cosine Delta would be the angle α. Evert *et al.* (2017) found that Cosine Delta, originally introduced by Smith and Aldridge (2011), is superior to the other ones as well as more robust when increasing or decreasing the number of features considered.

The fact that Cosine Delta performs better than classic Delta is crucial for our understanding of its mechanisms. When the measure of distance between two vectors is the angle, then their length does not matter. For example, if the *A* point was not (1, 5) but another point on the imaginary continuation of that same line, say (2, 10), then the distance between *A* and *B* would be the same because the angle between the vectors would not change. Because Cosine Delta outperforms other types of Delta we can infer that the *lengths* of the vectors do not matter (e.g. whether the author of *A* uses *the* much more often than the author of *B*) as much as their *orientation* in relation to each other, or the angle that they form (e.g. the fact that the author of *A* uses *the* more frequently than the average and *of* less frequently while *B* does the opposite). This leads Evert *et al.* (2017) to formulate the following hypothesis:

> *Key Profiles Hypothesis:* authors are distinguished by the overall pattern of variation of all features in relation to the norm and not by the magnitude of these variations.

To test this hypothesis, Evert *et al.* (2017) transformed all 'above average' z-scores to +1, all 'below average' z-scores to −1, and all values in between to 0. By doing that, they removed any effect of the length of the vectors. Because this operation consistently made all other Deltas almost as good as Cosine Delta, Evert *et al.* (2017) concluded that there is strong evidence for the key profiles hypothesis. An important implication of this hypothesis is that when it comes to authorship analysis it is not just a few remarkable features that matter but rather the patterning of the conjunction of many features that by themselves are not necessarily distinctive. It is the profile of the covariation that makes them distinctive, not their own single magnitude.

This conclusion is rather significant and, despite being purely mathematical, it advances our understanding of Delta. Accepting the Key Profiles Hypothesis means that given a multidimensional space of (function) words, each individual has its own place in it based on the pattern of over- or under-used (function)

---

[1] www.gutenberg.org/.

words. This is a fascinating picture yet it is not a full explanation because there are no immediately obvious *linguistic* reasons for the existence of these key profiles.

1.2.2 Explaining Authorship Analysis

It is fair to conclude that, in modern times, authorship analysis has become a subfield of computer science. Most of the articles on the subject are found in computer science conference proceedings and especially in the proceedings of the annual PAN conference, where competitions on various authorship problems are held.[2] In contrast, research published in linguistics is much more limited, both in scope and quantity (e.g. Chaski, 2001; Grant, 2007; Turell and Gavaldà, 2013; Wright, 2017).

The problem with authorship analysis being a branch of computer science is that this community is less interested in explanations and understanding and more keen on finding an automatic computational solution (Daelemans, 2013; Kestemont, 2014). The PAN competition leads the participants to focus on improving the accuracy of methods, which often tends to happen at the expense of explicability. For example, the most recent edition at the time of writing focused on verification and demonstrated that deep learning architectures can be very effective in solving this problem. However, the organisers also found that these methods do indeed exploit topic information (Kestemont *et al.*, 2020). Not being able to understand why a certain identification is made, with the risk that this is based on topic information, can be problematic for forensic applications (see Narayanan *et al.*'s (2012) criticism of Koppel *et al.*'s (2009, 2011) highly topic-sensitive feature selection).

The problem with the focus being on performance is that 'explanation' papers, even the ones concerned with mathematical explanations such as Argamon (2008) or Evert *et al.* (2017), are not common enough. One of the important exceptions is Kestemont (2014), who addressed the efficacy of function words. Function words are often selected because of their high frequency, their belonging to a closed set, their obliviousness to genre or topic, and their unconscious processing. Kestemont (2014), however, points out how decades of research in register variation have demonstrated that function words, which are lexical expressions of grammar, are not at all oblivious to genre (Biber, 1988; Biber and Conrad, 2009) but that, indeed, it is quite the opposite: all things being equal, function words' sensitivity to genre outweighs their sensitivity to an authorial signal (Mikros and Argiri, 2007). Kestemont (2014) also explains how, although there is evidence that readers process

---

[2] https://pan.webis.de/.

function words below the level of consciousness, it is unclear if the same applies to production. Finally, Kestemont (2014) proposes that the known efficacy of short character n-grams could be due to their capturing of both function words and grammatical morphemes, a hypothesis for which Sapkota *et al.* (2015) found strong support. Kestemont (2014) therefore concludes that the key to authorship analysis lies in those linguistic items that perform a function, called *functors* in psycholinguistics.

After decades of studies, this conclusion is an undeniable fact: frequency of functors contains authorial information, which therefore means that *individuals differ in the frequency with which they use functors*. The problem with this conclusion, which potentially is enough for computer scientists as an explanation, is that it actually does not make much *linguistic* sense on its own. Individuals cannot possibly vary in the frequency of use of functors because they prefer one over another. Individuals who use *the* more frequently than others do not do so because they like this word. And although we could attempt to justify the authorship signal of functors by saying that what distinguishes authors is the frequency with which they employ those functions expressed by the functors, in reality only very few functors have one and only one precise function (e.g. *that* can be a complementiser, a relative pronoun, a demonstrative, or a demonstrative pronoun). To get to the bottom of this, we must remember that *functors are the way that grammar manifests itself in characters that can be read by a computer*. Therefore, the interpretation of their success in identifying authors can only make sense if we instead shift our attention to the real phenomenon they are a proxy for: *grammar*.

This conclusion, however, reveals another covert assumption of computer science research on authorship analysis: although these studies appear to be completely atheoretical in their conception of language, they are not. Calculating the frequency of words in a text, where a word is defined as a string surrounded by punctuation or white spaces, assumes that words are the units of language production. Taking the relative frequency of a (function) word means measuring the probability of occurrence of a word on the assumption that the writer makes a choice when they select a word for every word in the text. This is a theory of linguistic production that is untenable in light of what we know about language processing.

These concerns have already been highlighted several years ago by Lancashire (1997, 2010), who suggested that we should go back to findings from neuroscience and cognitive psychology to understand an author's language, including the fact that we do not produce language word by word. He writes: 'we speak and write in chunks. If so, should we not pay as much attention to identifying an author's repeating phrases and collocational clusters as in calculating the frequency and whereabouts of an author's single words?' (Lancashire, 1997, p. 180). These ideas have, however, mostly been ignored by work in authorship analysis, possibly because the frequency of multi-word units has been found to be not very effective. For example, inspired by Lancashire's proposals, Antonia *et al.* (2014) found that the frequency of word n-grams can be a useful feature but often looking at single words is good enough. Many other computational studies over time have also reached the same conclusions and shown that single words or short character n-grams are simply far superior to any other feature, leading to the neglect of features larger than single words.

Finally, another wrong assumption often explicitly made in computer science papers is the apparent contrast between *content* and *style*, where 'the style factor of a text is considered orthogonal to its topic' (Stamatatos, 2009, p. 10). This assumption, which again appears to be common sense and atheoretical, is actually revealing of an underlying model of language production where a text is like a picture which conveys a meaning with its style being a purely aesthetic filter. This model implies that we can take a text (a picture), remove or isolate the meaning, and then extract the style (the filter). However, this process is again in contradiction with what we know about how language works. Style is a fairly complex concept inextricably linked to *register* (Biber and Conrad, 2009). It is more realistic to think about style as the interaction of an individual or social group with a particular situation but not as the *addition* of two orthogonal phenomena.

In conclusion, the linguistic explanations underlying existing methods of authorship analysis can only be found using plausible theories of language processing. The connection between authorship analysis and linguistics cannot be broken, in the same way that biology and chemistry cannot be ignored by the computational techniques used to create DNA profiles. In the present work, a theory connecting authorship analysis to modern cognitive and psycholinguistic findings is established. Before introducing this theory, the rest of the section explains the necessary foundational concepts borrowed from cognitive linguistics.

1.3 Fundamentals of Cognitive Linguistics

A framework for linguistically realistic authorship analysis should meet two desiderata: (1) it must be able to handle real-life language usage; and (2) it must be scientifically plausible, meaning that it should be consistent with other well-established facts about the human mind. The proposal put forward in the present work is that these desiderata are met by *usage-based linguistics* and, more specifically, *cognitive linguistics*.

Firstly, what is needed for authorship analysis is a theory of language that can explain usage events. Therefore, purely formal and idealised frameworks such as mainstream generative grammar, which by definition rejects the study of usage, must be excluded. This is not a value judgement: such a framework is clearly designed for purposes that do not match the reality of dealing with language in use. In contrast, cognitive linguistics subscribes to Beckner *et al.*'s (2009) main tenet that language is a *complex adaptive system* from which the structures of language emerge spontaneously out of individuals' interactions in context. This in turn means that studies in cognitive linguistics are always concerned with and oriented towards language usage.

Secondly, authorship analysis should be based as much as possible on models of language that see language as a property of the human mind because, ultimately, the act of text creation is a process that happens in the mind of the author. Thus, the optimal point of departure for a science of authorship analysis must be what is currently known about language production. Different varieties of cognitive linguistics meet this desideratum because they subscribe to the *Cognitive Commitment* to 'make one's account of human language accord with what is generally known about the mind and the brain' (Lakoff, 1990, p. 40).

Among the various frameworks or theories that can be classified as cognitive linguistics we can name Cognitive Grammar (Langacker, 1987), Construction Grammar (Goldberg, 1995, 2003, 2006), the theory of Lexical Priming (Hoey, 2005), Word Grammar (Hudson, 1996, 2010), and Radical Construction Grammar (Croft, 2001). In the rest of this section, I will outline four key foundational concepts that cognitive linguistics usage-based frameworks agree on and that are useful to build the foundations for a theory of individuality for authorship analysis, which is then introduced in Section 2.

1.3.1 Lexis and Grammar Are Inseparable

One of the key foundational concepts of most usage-based, functional, and cognitive linguistics frameworks is the treatment of lexis and grammar as a unified entity called *lexicogrammar*. Usage-based linguistics rejects the notion that the lexicon provides the building blocks of sentences that are then in turn combined using the rules of grammar. Instead, these frameworks propose that grammar and the lexicon are on a continuum. This conclusion emerges from decades of research on language use. When real language is studied in context, the strong division between grammar and lexis becomes hard to justify. For example, research in corpus linguistics has demonstrated that the 'rules of grammar' that apply generically to any lexical item belonging to a certain morphosyntactic category are very rare. Instead, lexical items are often co-selected and form structures with open slots that can be filled according to sometimes highly idiosyncratic constraints. This evidence comes from various areas, such as formulaic language (e.g. Schmitt, 2004; Wray, 2008; Biber, 2009), the idiosyncratic constraints on verb arguments (e.g. Goldberg, 1995; Ellis *et al.*, 2016), research on grammaticalisation (e.g. Bybee, 2006), or studies on collocations (e.g. Sinclair, 1991; Gries, 2013). These conclusions have been reached in several functional or usage-based linguistic theories, such as systemic functional linguistics (Halliday and Matthiessen, 2004), pattern grammar (Hunston and Francis, 2000), and all the cognitive linguistics frameworks mentioned in the previous section.

The important consequence of this discovery for authorship analysis, as explained before, is that it is not cognitively realistic to treat words as the basic unit of linguistic choice. Although descriptively we can identify and study these units, this does not mean that the units are also cognitively realistic for a model of language production. Real data instead suggests that any authorship analysis study or system that assumes that authors choose words one by one according to the rules of grammar is actually not scientifically plausible.

1.3.2 Language Is Processed in Chunks

Evidence from corpora has demonstrated that a lot of the language we produce is formulaic and recycled. For example, Erman and Warren (2000) estimated that about 55 per cent of choices in a text are prefabricated and that the average length of non-prefabricated strings is around three or four words. To make sense of this empirical fact, Sinclair (1991) proposed that linguistic production happens according to two principles of composition: the *Idiom Principle* and the *Open Choice Principle*, a process for which there is neurocognitive evidence (Ullman, 2004, 2013). When confronted with a linguistic production task, speakers do not generate sentences from scratch but they have a set of prefabricated idioms that they use whenever possible and only resort to original composition when necessary. Thus, Sinclair's theory suggests that memory plays a much bigger role than expected in language processing, a proposal that is consistent with our understanding of other areas of human cognition. Recent advances in neuroscience suggest that the computational analogy of a memory (the hard disk) and a processor (the CPU) does not really apply to the brain, where memory cannot be separated from processing (Dasgupta and Gershman, 2021; Fedorenko, 2021). Neurons can only store memories and processing can be thought of as the activation of these memories (Hasson *et al.*, 2015).

In cognitive psychology, memory is classified as short term or long term. In turn, long-term memory can be *declarative*, which is conscious memory of mostly things like facts and events, or *procedural*, which is unconscious memory of things like skills and habits (Divjak, 2019). What is called *automatisation* of a behaviour is the storing of results of previous processing as units instead of reprocessing them from scratch (Dasgupta and Gershman, 2021) and long-term memories of this kind are real and physical changes in the brain, although their exact nature is not yet clear (Divjak, 2019). The processing of language is strictly connected to procedural memory and this makes sense if we think of our mental grammar being an emergent generalisation of routinised behaviour strengthened by use until it becomes unconscious, in a fashion similar to other procedural skills like driving (Diessel, 2019, p. 34). These considerations explain why a lot of language is recycled: speakers rely on ritualised and automatised behaviour which is stored as a trace in long-term memory.

The importance of automatisation as the core of language processing is an insight that was incorporated in the seminal work of Langacker's Cognitive Grammar very early on. Langacker (1987, p. 57) defined the most basic linguistic unit of processing as a linguistic structure that a speaker can process automatically. Although Langacker (1987) does not explicitly mention it, what he proposed matches the well-established cognitive psychology concept of a *chunk* (Gobet *et al.*, 2001). The notion of *chunking* was introduced by Miller (1956), who discovered that human short-term memory can contain at maximum 7 ($\pm$ 2) items, although this has been more recently revised to 4 (Cowan, 2001).

Miller (1956) argued that human memory can work around this constraint by chunking the input. For example, let's consider this sequence of 26 characters:

csroosmlaoenwrcoevrreyalpm.

If the reader were asked to recollect it all from memory, this would be a very hard task. However, any English speaker would be able to recollect from memory the following sequence of the same 26 characters reordered:

classroomownerrecoverylamp.

The reason we can remember the 26 characters only in this order is that we chunk them into four words and keep those in memory, rather than the single characters, thus overcoming our working memory constraint. This example, adapted from McCauley and Christiansen (2015), is a clear demonstration of how chunking works as an information compression strategy for the brain (Divjak, 2019). Chunking also leads to the emergence of abstractions in the form of *templates*; that is, schematic chunks that contain open slots where other chunks can be inserted. This mechanism, which is fundamental for most human cognition, is what leads to the creation of grammatical constructions (Gobet *et al.*, 2001).

Although several cognitive linguistic theories discuss the important role of chunking in language processing (e.g. Ellis, 2002; Bybee, 2010), the most prominent is Christiansen and Chater's (2016) Now-or-Never Bottleneck theory of language processing. This theory argues that, because the flow of information in input and output is very fast and our working memory is fleeting, language processing must rely on chunking to compress information at increasingly high levels of complexity to bypass this information bottleneck. In comprehension, a sound stream can be initially chunked into phoneme clusters, then recognised as words, words chunked in phrases, phrases in sentences, and so on. Once an item is chunked, this is passed on to a higher level of abstraction where this chunk counts as one unit, so essentially compressing the information and bypassing the short-term memory constraints.

On the other hand, in production, the theory proposes that the same process happens in reverse. Starting from units at the level of discourse, the meaning is produced at a certain level of abstraction and realised as automatised chunks at a level below until reaching articulatory gestures. This model of production implies that our planning is far less elaborated than we might intuitively think. Micro-decisions about words or phrases only happen long after the overall discourse plan has been put in place by the speaker, a fact consistent with psycholinguistic evidence (Christiansen and Chater, 2016, p. 6).

The more abstract a chunk is, the more likely it is that it is a combination of lower-level chunks. For example, a hypothetical chunk representing a transitive declarative sentence in English, [N V N], is made up of three units that are themselves abstract chunks made of chunks at the level of words (what we would traditionally call a noun/verb phrase), which in turn are made up of other chunks (character or sound clusters). This way of understanding processing explains the formation of novel expressions following something that we imagine as 'rules': existing template chunks are used as models to build new expressions.

In sum, language is processed in both comprehension and production in units called chunks, which can be made up of articulatory gestures, phoneme clusters, words, multi-word units, and so on, with some of them serving as templates to generate new formulations in what Sinclair would call the Open Choice Principle of composition.

We can therefore imagine the lexicogrammar of a language as a repository of units, from what we normally call a word (e.g. *dog*) to a morpheme (e.g. *-ness*) to highly schematic rules, like the order of subject and verb, and everything in between (e.g. *the* X-*er the* Y-*er*), including highly automatised forms that are not treated as units in traditional grammar (e.g. *I don't know if*).

From a cognitive point of view, therefore, the lexicogrammar is more similar to the traditional view of a lexicon than to a list of rules. This over-reliance on memory is responsible for the fact that, as proposed by Sinclair, speakers resort to the Open Choice Principle exclusively when necessary. This effect is called *pre-emption*: speakers block novel formulations if an alternative acceptable formulation already exists, tending to judge the novel formulations as ungrammatical or unacceptable (e.g. **warmness* vs *warmth*, **explain me this* vs *explain this to me*) (Goldberg, 2019). The reason for this pre-emption is at least twofold: part of it is due to the cognitive burden of creating something new but part of it is linked to the sociocognitive constraints that lead us to judge something unnecessarily novel as 'wrong'.

1.3.3 Units Are Formed and Strengthened through Entrenchment and Conventionalisation

The repeated usage of form units in context leads to the formation of new units through a process called *entrenchment* (Langacker, 1987, p. 59). We can imagine entrenchment as the strengthening of the connection between two already existing units or between a unit and a context, a process that happens mostly via repetition, which allows enough neural activity to lead to those physical changes in the brain that constitute long-term memory (Divjak, 2019). The more entrenched two existing units are, the more these are readily recognised by a speaker and therefore become a new unit. Similarly, the more entrenched an existing unit becomes in a particular context, the more this will be associated with its semantic-pragmatic function in that context. In both cases, the more entrenched a relation is, the more this is accessible to be used and recognised as 'acceptable' or 'grammatical' by an individual (Goldberg, 2019, p. 60). This mechanism also explains the creation of new grammatical constructions in a language over time (Bybee, 2006, 2010).

However, because language is both a property of an individual and a property of a community, the mechanism of mental entrenchment is not enough to explain the way we achieve agreement on what linguistic units count as such and what they mean. The additional component needed is the process of *conventionalisation*. Schmid's (2015) *Entrenchment-and-Conventionalisation Model* proposes that the relationship between these two concepts is what links an individual's mental lexicogrammar to the lexicogrammar of a speech community. The repetition of linguistic patterns leads to both the entrenchment of this knowledge in the linguistic individual's mind and its conventionalisation in a community of individuals sustained through repeated linguistic interaction. The combination of these two processes and their reinforcing feedback loop leads to our conception of language as a fixed entity with rules we all agree on.

Another way to describe this process is as a 'phenomenon of the third kind' or an 'invisible hand phenomenon' where the final result is an emergent unintentional product of human interaction (Dąbrowska (2020), following Keller (1994)). The emergence of linguistic units through entrenchment and conventionalisation is like the emergence of paths in a field or forest: the more often a route is taken, the more the route becomes easy to take and thus it is used more often by members of the community until it becomes the preferred default road to reach a certain place. Although no member of the community set up to create a path, this nonetheless naturally emerges through the repeated actions of the community motivated by other goals.

1.3.4 Grammar Is a Network

Finally, another notion largely agreed upon by many if not all cognitive usage-based linguistic frameworks is that knowledge of language is a network (Langacker, 1987; Goldberg, 1995; Croft, 2001; Bybee, 2010; Hudson, 2010; Hilpert, 2014; Diessel, 2019). The way memory organises any kind of knowledge is by forming hierarchies of connected units (Bybee, 2010, p. 35). Therefore, although previously the lexicogrammar was called a 'repertoire', this is not completely true because the lexicogrammatical units are not stored in isolation but are instead connected to each other so that associations between them are built (Goldberg, 2019, pp. 51–6). We can therefore imagine a lexicogrammar as a network where the units, or *chunks*, are the nodes and the vertices are the relationships between them. These relationships can be vertical or taxonomic (e.g. unit X is a type of unit Y) but also horizontal, as, for example, the relationship between the active and passive voice constructions. Lexicogrammar is therefore organised in a very similar way to how the mental lexicon is traditionally conceptualised.

1.4 Idiolect and Linguistic Individuality

Before moving on to the outlining of a theory of individuality, this section reviews the available theories and evidence regarding individuality and uniqueness in language. This topic is not something that has been thoroughly investigated in linguistics and the reason for this gap is understandable. For the scientific study of human language to progress, it is natural that the focus at first should be on what is shared across individuals rather than on differences and uniqueness. Although linguists from different theoretical standpoints tacitly agree that each person has their own *idiolect*, a notion first introduced by Bloch (1948) indicating a personal variety of a language, the magnitude of these differences has simply not been investigated so far. Indeed, until very recent modern work that will be reviewed below, individual differences have largely been ignored in linguistics. This is a similar situation to cognitive science more generally. Kidd *et al.* (2018, p. 154), for example, comment that the large individual differences in cognition are 'an inconvenient truth': although we know that they exist, we treat them as noise in the data in order to generalise our findings.

Among the first systematic theoretical accounts of individuality and idiolect in language for the purpose of authorship analysis is McMenamin (2002). In his theory, McMenamin (2002, p. 53) explains that 'no two individuals use and perceive language in exactly the same way' as the result of the fact that language is a *discrete combinatorial system* (Pinker, 1994). Language, like DNA, combines smaller units to create larger ones and this process, which is highly combinatorial, leads to an incredibly large number of possible choices. Individuality and uniqueness are therefore a consequence of this combinatorial explosion. However, although this is a promising point of departure, McMenamin (2002) does not explain why combinatorics should necessarily lead to linguistic individuality and uniqueness. The fact that choices are available does not imply that all of them are selected nor that all individuals must make consistently different choices. McMenamin (2002) only assumes that this is the case: individuals make repeated choices that, in turn, form their own styles, which can be studied using methods from the discipline of *stylistics*.

McMenamin's stylistics approach was strongly criticised by Chaski (2001), who instead argued that the reason why individuals are linguistically unique is rooted in their personalised mental grammar. As a consequence, reliable authorship analysis can only be carried out by looking at the syntactic structures produced by individuals. This *syntactic* (sometimes also called *cognitive*) theory of authorship analysis, however, is arguably not substantiated by either theoretical or empirical work. Firstly, Chaski (2001) does not explain why mental syntactic representations should be different across individuals. Secondly, more than twenty years of research in computational authorship analysis have demonstrated that it is indeed entirely possible to carry out successful authorship analysis work without using any a priori notion of syntactic structure.

In contrast, although Chaski's (2001) approach has been sometimes labelled as 'cognitive', the explanations put forward by McMenamin (2002) are much more consistent with the cognitive usage-based approach and with the state of the art of psychological understanding of how language works than Chaski's (2001). As explained by Nini and Grant (2013), the differences in syntactic structures detected by Chaski (2001) could still be explained by each individual's unique history of linguistic usage events as proposed by McMenamin (2002).

The origin of individuality within the stylistic approach is addressed by Turell's (2010) concept of *idiolectal style*. This theory explains that individuality is not the result of different repertoires but of different selections of items within the space of possibilities offered by a language. This notion of idiolectal style is consistent with Nini and Grant's (2013) argument based on Halliday's Systemic Functional Linguistics, where an idiolect is theorised to be formed by the habitual choices in the various linguistic systems of a language. Nini and Grant (2013) thus agree with Turell (2010) and add that the reason for this individuality lies in the uniqueness of the sociolinguistic history of an individual.

The most recent theoretical advancement linking individuality in language to sociolinguistics is put forward by Grant and MacLeod's (2020) *Resource-Constraint Theory of Identity*. Following Johnstone (1996), they maintain that identity is not a property of the individual but of the interaction between the individual and the situation. An identity is not a static attribute of a person but an action or a performance that cannot be found in isolation. Thus, a person's language is not just the product of their sociolinguistic profile but is actively constituted by the choices they make in a situation. This performance of identity is, however, not unconstrained because it is limited by the linguistic resources belonging to an individual's repertoire, which in turn depend on their sociolinguistic history. This repertoire is mutable and changes over time, following the individual's language change.

Another theoretical perspective is provided by Coulthard (2004, p. 431), who proposed that 'every native speaker has their own distinct and individual version of the language they speak and write' and that 'this *idiolect* will manifest itself through distinctive and idiosyncratic choices'. Similarly to McMenamin (2002), therefore, Coulthard (2004) explains that the locus of individuality is choice and, more specifically, the *combination* of choices. He proposes that *idiolectal co-selection* leads to a high level of idiosyncrasies that resemble a *linguistic fingerprint*, even though he discourages this analogy. A famous example of the power of idiolectal co-selection is the analysis of the Unabomber's writings, where a list of twelve linguistic items (e.g. *at any rate, clearly, presumably, thereabouts*) uniquely connected the Unabomber's manifesto to an article written by Ted Kaczynski (Coulthard *et al.*, 2017). In other words, then, Coulthard (2004) connects individuality and uniqueness to the combinatorics of language, although, unlike McMenamin (2002), he does not connect this phenomenon to *style*. Similarly to McMenamin (2002), however, Coulthard does not provide an explanation as to why individuals should differ in their co-selections.

Empirical validation for Coulthard's (2004, 2013) proposal was found in the analysis of lexical n-grams in the Enron corpus, a large corpus of emails collected after the collapse of the American company Enron. Wright (2013) looked at a sub-sample of four members of this community and discovered that some authors can be extremely distinctive in their combination of choices of greetings and farewells when compared to a similar population of 126 other authors. Then, Wright (2017) demonstrated how something seemingly common, such as the word sequences '*a clean and redlined version*' or '*please review and let's discuss*', is unique to a particular author. Even though other similar authors express the same meaning repeatedly in the corpus, they choose formulations that are similar but not identical to those. Using a subset of twelve demographically similar authors, Wright (2017) showed that it is possible to use the presence/absence of word n-grams to attribute even relatively short emails in a cohort of 175 candidates. Wright (2017) connects these findings to the notions of cognitive linguistics introduced above and he therefore proposes an explanation for Coulthard's (2004) idiolectal co-selection phenomenon: individuality emerges from consistent and repeated usage of a certain sequence of words to realise a speech act, a process leading to this sequence becoming entrenched for that person.

Coulthard's (2004) and McMenamin's (2002) ideas can therefore be connected to usage-based cognitive linguistic frameworks described in the previous section. Most of or all the cognitive linguistic frameworks indirectly predict that linguistic individuality exists and that its effect on language should be notable. Because the central argument of these frameworks is that the linguistic system is formed through use and experience, individuals must be highly heterogenous and, indeed, unique in the version of their language that they know. For example, Langacker (1987, p. 62) suggested that, 'no two speakers control precisely the same set of units [. . .] even if their speech patterns appear to be identical' and that 'the set of units mastered by all members of a speech community might be a rather small proportion of the units constituting the linguistic ability of any given speaker', a position supported by Schmid (2015, p. 16), who explains how this is a consequence of entrenchment, which is a highly personal phenomenon.

Even though none of the studies reviewed so far explicitly set out to test the predictions of cognitive linguistics, cumulatively there is enough work that constitutes indirect evidence that there is a substantial amount of individuality in language, especially when considering research on authorship analysis.

Another research strand that is important to consider for individuality is the cognitive linguistic research on language acquisition. It is well established that there are substantial and pervasive individual differences both in the acquisition of our first language and in adulthood and that these individual differences depend on both environmental and cognitive factors, such as individual differences in working memory, executive functions, and statistical learning (Kidd *et al.*, 2018; Kidd *et al.*, 2020). Of particular note in the context of adults' grammar differences is the work of Dąbrowska (2012, 2015, 2018), who presents evidence that native speakers of a language do not necessarily acquire all its core grammatical constructions or reach the same conclusions about how to use them. Because individuals possess different combinations of cognitive attributes, even with identical exposure the grammar they arrive at could be quite different. For example, Dąbrowska (2015) reports how native speakers of English who are not well educated do not know how to process grammatical constructions that are more frequent in written registers that they are less familiar with, such as sentences with parasitic gaps, quantifiers, or even the passive voice. Dąbrowska's (2015) conclusion, in line with cognitive linguistic proposals, is that even though it appears as if all members of a community share the same grammar, this is not really the case.

In addition to experiments, cognitive linguistic research using corpora has also shown that linguistic individuality is strong. De Smet (2016) was among the first studies to show how to use corpora to test hypotheses about individual authors' cognition and, in recent times, this approach has grown considerably, especially in historical linguistics (e.g. Schmid and Mantlik, 2015). Research in this area is growing fast, with studies such as Petré and Van de Velde (2018), Anthonissen and Petré (2019), and Fonteyn and Nini (2020) all finding that individual differences are substantial and cannot be simply reduced to noise.

In parallel, more evidence of a high degree of individuality in language is also found using synchronic data. A study by Mollin (2009) on the language of former British Prime Minister Tony Blair uncovered evidence that collocations can be highly idiosyncratic. Similarly, Barlow (2013) found that White House press secretaries can be very distinctive in their language, despite the similarities in their linguistic tasks. Another more recent example is Schmid *et al.* (2021), who uncovered strong individual variation in the way the construction [*that's* ADJ] is used, both in terms of the adjective selected and in its pragmatic function. Evidence of chunking being idiosyncratic therefore leading to different and unique repertoires was found by Vetchinnikova (2017) after discovering that there exist more fixed sequences in corpora of single individuals than in corpora containing language from multiple individuals, a finding indirectly replicated on a larger scale by Dunn and Nini (2021).

In sum, it is fair to conclude that individual variation in language is present and is extensive. The large effects found in these studies cannot be attributed to just noise in the data as the findings come from the two complementary perspectives of experimental and corpus studies. For this reason, the development of a Theory of Linguistic Individuality that is based on foundational concepts and assumptions of usage-based cognitive linguistics is licensed and desirable in order to inform both research and practice in authorship analysis. This formal Theory of Linguistic Individuality is the object of the next section.

2 Formal Grounding for a Theory of Linguistic Individuality

2.1 Introduction

Firstly, it is important to clarify that the term *theory* is here intended in its scientific sense of a set of principles and laws based on commonly agreed and verifiable facts that form a coherent explanation of a phenomenon. A theory generates hypotheses which in turn lead to empirically verifiable predictions. If these predictions are correct, then the theory is a good model of reality. If not, the theory must be changed accordingly or, in case its foundations are demolished by the evidence, abandoned altogether in favour of another competing theory.

To the best of my knowledge, there are no formal theories of linguistic individuality or idiolect, let alone theories that are specifically tailored to being applied to authorship analysis. This includes Grant and MacLeod's (2020) *Resource-Constraint Theory of Identity*, which is not a theory of linguistic individuality but a theory of how individuals use their repertoire of resources to perform a linguistic identity in a communicative situation. Grant and MacLeod (2020) do not explain how and why individuals possess repertoires that are possibly unique to them at a certain point in time. Instead, the theory that is outlined in this section is focused precisely on this aspect and it can be therefore thought of as complementary to Grant and MacLeod (2020).

As detailed in Section 1.4, several important theoretical points have been made and a body of evidence has been gradually accumulated over the years on linguistic individuality but there has not yet been an attempt to tie all these threads together. The present theory is an attempt to ground all the previous proposals and evidence on what we already know about language processing from the point of view of cognitive science using the foundational notions presented in Section 1.3. The goal of this section and of this Element is therefore to introduce a theory of linguistic individuality that starts from scientifically plausible and established notions of language processing to then build on top of these the foundations for a linguistically and scientifically valid authorship analysis.

2.2 Basic Definitions

2.2.1 Linguistic Units

Following mainly Langacker (1987) but also Christiansen and Chater (2016) and Gobet *et al.* (2001), the most basic unit of linguistic processing is defined as in Definition 1.

Definition 1. A piece of linguistic information is called a *linguistic unit* [*u*] for an individual *A* if this is stored in *A*'s long-term memory so that *A* can produce [*u*] automatically.

This definition is therefore very similar if not identical to the definition of a chunk in cognitive psychology.

Linguistic units can but do not have to correspond to traditional grammar units or to constructions combining a complete meaning with a complete form. For example, [*ing*] is probably an important unit for all speakers of English and it corresponds to the traditional grammar category of morphemes, which then corresponds to certain functions/meanings. However, clusters such as [*adv*], [*blo*], or [*spr*] are also units despite their lack of meaning. They make up what is known as the phonotactics of English, which is what makes a certain word 'sound English'. Larger sequences of characters or sounds can be what we normally call words, such as [*follow*], but also multi-word units, [*follow up*], as long as they are automatic for an individual. This means that, as for sequences of sounds or characters, combinations of words can count as units even if they do not correspond to traditional grammatical categories. A highly frequent and predictable sequence such as [*I don't know if*] is likely to be a unit for many speakers of English.

Units must be combined to create novel utterances, leading to the creation of *structures*.

Definition 2. A combination of units, $\langle [u_1][u_2] \rangle$, is called a *structure* for individual *A* if it is not stored in *A*'s long-term memory.

For example, [*How are you?*] is probably a unit for most speakers of English despite the fact that it could be decomposed as a combination of smaller units. This is because this sentence can be reproduced effortlessly and automatically for a speaker as a single item. If, however, a hypothetical speaker of English were to be unfamiliar with this sentence, then they would consider it a novel structure made of smaller units, thus $\langle [How][are][you][?] \rangle$. Although both versions, as a unit or as a structure, can be produced by a speaker capable of doing so, speakers will always try to recur to the longest most complete stored unit when possible rather than creating a structure every time (see Section 1.3.2).

Abstractions over units are possible and lead to the creation of *categories*, which are the variable slots in the special types of chunks called *templates*, such as [Noun *gives* Noun *to* Noun][3] (see Section 1.3.2 and Gobet *et al.*, 2001). These

---

[3] Categories from traditional grammar are only used for convenience. In reality, as explained above, these abstractions emerge from usage and might or might not correspond to traditional grammatical categories.

templates can be very general, and roughly correspond to categories such as the traditional 'noun', or very restricted, such as paradigms like *be/is/are*.

Most importantly, units do not have to be sequences and can be, for example, discontinuous or unordered collocations of lexical items, as long as their co-occurrence is predictable enough for the individual that they can produce them automatically. Thus, [MAKE MISTAKE], where capital letters are used to indicate lemmas, is a unit because these two words are highly predictable, even though the final produced output could either be *I made a mistake* or *mistakes were made*.

Finally, it is important to stress that units do not belong to a language but to an individual. Although there might be many units shared by all or almost all speakers of a language, fundamentally units are idiosyncratic and personal. For example, [*nowt*] is likely to be a unit only for certain speakers of English that are from specific regions; that is, what we call a dialect. Units could be connected to social groups. For example, the famous sequence [*I then*] was a crucial piece of evidence of police interference in both the Evans statements case (Svartvik, 1968) and in the Derek Bentley case (Coulthard *et al.*, 2017), the reason being that this is a unit for police officers. Ultimately, units are idiosyncratic, and these are manifested in combinations that are potentially unique to a single individual. An example of that could be the [KEEP *letter back till I*] found in the Jack the Ripper letters (Nini 2018), or [*a clean and redlined version*] or [*please review and let's discuss*] (Wright 2017) (see Section 1.4).

2.2.2 Grammar

As explained in Section 1.3, in cognitive linguistics a person's lexicogrammar (or more simply grammar from now on) is seen as a network of units, similar to the left-hand side set in Figure 2 below. Grammars can therefore be represented mathematically as graphs, which are pairs such as:

$$G = (V, E)$$

where both V and E are *sets*, the first one of *nodes* and the second one of *edges*.

In this work, the model is simplified by assuming that the grammar of an individual is just the set of nodes, V. In other words, as shown in Figure 2, we can remove the links that connect the units and pretend that the grammar of a person is just an unstructured repository. The set representation is a simplification where we maintain the composition of the elements of the grammar but we remove the connection across these elements for the purpose of simplicity.

This view of the grammar of a person as a finite set of units that they can produce automatically is not unrealistic because, although we can and we do

create novel utterances all the time, the set of units we use to make them is
dependent on our repertoire, which depends on our memory, which in turn is
finite. If we can imagine the grammar of a person as a set, then we can use the
notations and tools from another area of discrete mathematics, *set theory*. Thus,
the example set in Figure 2 of the grammar *G* of an individual *A*, which we call
G^A, would be:

$$G^A = \{[\textit{on the other hand,}], \; [\textit{the N of}], \; [\text{P N}], \; [\textit{hope}], \; [\text{A,}], \; \ldots\}$$

where each element of the set is separated by a comma and each unit is
contained in square brackets.

In reality, this way of representing grammar as a set of units is somewhat
comparable to the traditional representation of grammar as a list of rules. Chunks
can indeed be equated to rules because, for example, the word-punctuation unit
[*and,*] could be described as the rule of using a comma after the coordinator *and*.
Any complex unit is, in essence, a rule for how to order or combine sub-units over
time (see Section 1.3.2 and Christiansen and Chater, 2016).

This definition is, however, incomplete because it does not take entrenchment
into account. As Langacker (1987, p. 59) suggests, it is not realistic to assume that
there is a hard boundary of entrenchment that makes something a unit for an
individual. Instead, it is better to think of units as standing on a continuum of
various levels of entrenchment. Something that an author uses more often is more
entrenched for them than something that the author almost never uses, even though
they are still able to understand it. This is probably what leads to some strings or
sentences being units for one person but novel structures for another person, even
though this second person can still understand what is being communicated.

Therefore, if we want to represent the grammar of a person as a set, a more
realistic model is one where this set is *fuzzy*. In mathematics, a fuzzy set is a set
where each element has a probability of belonging. Rather than, for example,

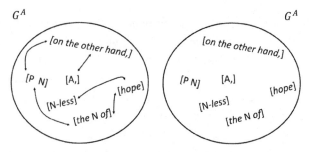

Figure 2 Graphical representation of a mental grammar as a set (right)
compared with a graph representation (left).

$A = \{a, b, c, \ldots\}$, a fuzzy set looks like $A = \{(a, 0.3), (b, 0.7), (c, 1), \ldots\}$, where each element is enclosed in round brackets containing both the element itself and its probability of belonging to the set. We can think of this probability of belonging as the mathematical formalisation of the concept of entrenchment and we can call it ε.

This model of grammar is pictured in Figure 3, where the dashed lines become more solid as entrenchment increases from a theoretical 0, meaning the person has never used a particular structure, which can therefore only be a unit for another person, to an ideal 1, meaning that the unit is maximally entrenched and the speaker produces it completely automatically.

As done before, however, although unit membership is continuous, for the sake of this work we can say that any unit with entrenchment above a certain threshold that we call π is an element of the grammar of an individual, thus a unit that they can automatically produce. Thus, the grammar of an individual A, G^A, is a set of units obtained by taking only those units for which $\varepsilon \geq \pi$. Because this threshold makes the membership discrete again (either a unit belongs to a grammar or not), then for simplicity we can treat G^A as a normal, non-fuzzy set.

This definition of grammar is still not complete, however, because an individual's grammar is not a static entity but one that changes over time, even in adulthood. Speakers constantly learn how to use new units and also *lose* units, depending on their usage and, consequently, the level of entrenchment.

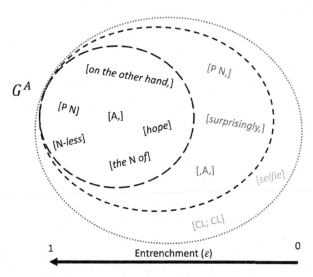

Figure 3 Graphical representation of a mental grammar with different degrees of entrenchment, from a theoretical 1 to a theoretical 0.

Therefore, time is an important and essential component to be added to the definition of a grammar, the final definition of which is Definition 3.

Definition 3. A grammar G of a person A at a time t, or G_t^A, is the set of units with entrenchment $\varepsilon \geq \pi$ for person A at time t.

The inclusion of time in the theory is also fundamental for authorship analysis. The fact that we can, at least theoretically, only observe a snapshot of a speaker's mental grammar at a particular time implies that authorship analysis cannot be equated to fingerprint or DNA identification because these two biological characteristics of a person's identity do not change over time.

2.2.3 Idiolect

This definition of grammar leads us to the definition of *idiolect*:

Definition 4. The idiolect I of a person A, or I^A, is an indexed family of grammars G_t^A for each time t, $I^A = \left(G_{t=1}^A, G_{t=2}^A \dots G_{t=n}^A\right)$.

In other words, Definition 4 sees idiolect as the *index set* of the grammars of a person throughout their lifetime. This definition is slightly different to Bloch's (1948, p. 7) famous definition of idiolect: 'the totality of the possible utterances of one speaker at one time in using a language to interact with one other speaker', which is instead more similar to the definition of an individual's grammar given in Definition 3.

This definition of idiolect is necessary because units can be both acquired and lost. For example, a person in their early childhood could acquire the unit [*where mummy*], which is then lost. Lost units are still part of the idiolect of this person, even though they might not be units for them at a particular point in time. Such a definition, apart from being cognitively realistic, is also convenient when dealing with historical data (e.g. Grieve *et al.*, 2019). In this way, a distinction is made between what an author can do at a certain time, which is their G_t, in contrast to their entire potential across their lifetime, their I.

2.2.4 Language and Variety

Because languages constantly evolve, it only makes sense to talk about languages at particular points in time. We therefore define a language as in Definition 5.

Definition 5. A language or variety L including N speakers at a particular point in time t, or L_t, is a fuzzy set of units $[u]$ with its membership function μ_L being the proportion of the N grammars G for which $[u] \in G$.

In simple words, a unit is deemed to be part of a language or variety to the extent that a number of its speakers have it in their grammar (with $\varepsilon > 0$). For example, if we say that in the community for language/variety L half of them have $[u]$ in their G_t, then $\mu_L([u]) = 0.5$. For English we can reasonably argue that $[the]$ is a unit that all speakers share. Thus, $\mu_{English}([the]) = 1$ because if we imagine the overlap of all the grammars of its speakers, then this is equal to the number of speakers. In contrast, $\mu_{English}([\,jg]) = 0$, because this is not a sequence of characters/sounds of English. Then, of course, there are many units that are units for only some people, for example $\mu_{English}([nowt]) = 0.02$ or $\mu_{English}([I\ then]) = 0.01$, where the numbers are just made-up examples that ideally would correspond to, respectively, the proportion of speakers of a certain dialect or a certain register. Therefore, dialects, sociolects, registers, or any variety can also be defined following Definition 5, the only change being how its speakers are defined.

An important consequence of defining a language or variety in this way is that units for just one person are part of the language/variety. However, this definition of a language is actually realistic for usage-based frameworks. As explained by Schmid's (2015) entrenchment-and-conventionalisation model and as also conceptualised by the view of language as a complex adaptive system, the individual's mind and the community are linked inextricably and what is a unit only held in the mind of one person today can become a unit that belongs to an entire community tomorrow.

We can imagine two different individuals' grammars embedded in a language L at a time t like in Figure 4.

This graphical representation shows how the theory outlined here predicts that there will be units that are shared by individuals and units that only certain individuals possess, as explained in the relevant section above. There will also be many units that none of the two individuals A and B considered in Figure 4 possess and that therefore are outside of both their grammars. However, these units must exist in the mental grammar of other individuals that are not represented in Figure 4 for convenience. In other words, any grammar at any point in time is a subset of the language at that point in time, $G_t \subset L_t$.

2.2.5 Text

So far, the definitions above have dealt with sets, fuzzy or discrete. A set is a mathematical object that is not constituted by elements that are repeated. Using corpus linguistics terminology, a set is made up of *types*, not *tokens*. For example, the set of words that make up the sentence 'the cat sat on the mat' is $S = \{the, cat, sat, on, mat\}$. Therefore, it does not matter how many times

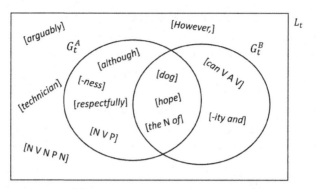

Figure 4 Graphical representation of the grammars of two individuals contextualised within a language at a particular time *t*.

a word is repeated in a text, the set of words used in that text would only include the types.

This is not, however, how texts, written or spoken, come about in everyday language. Units of all size and generality must be repeated to create a text. For this reason, texts must be modelled as *sequences*, as in Definition 6.

> **Definition 6.** A *text* produced by a person A at a time t, or T_t^A, is a sequence of characters or sounds generated using units elements of G_t^A.

Therefore, although T_t^A is not a set of units in itself, the information about the units that were used to generate it are present in the text and it can therefore be potentially transformed into a set using a *grammar induction function*, as defined in Definition 7.

> **Definition 7.** A *grammar induction function* $\gamma()$ is a function that takes as input one or more texts T_t^A produced by individual A and returns the G_t^A that generated it or an approximation to it, $\hat{G}_t^A$, thus $\gamma(T_t^A) = \hat{G}_t^A$, with $\hat{G}_t^A \subseteq G_t^A$.

Any set of units extracted from a text or corpus, which we can call $\hat{G}_t^A$, is likely to only be an approximation to the full grammar of the individual who produced it. However, this approximation must still be a subset of the actual G_t of the individual.

2.3 The Principle of Linguistic Individuality

After establishing the definitions above, it is now possible to use the vocabulary of the theory to express its most fundamental principle, the *Principle of Linguistic Individuality*:

> At any moment in time t, for any language L_t, there do not exist two individuals, A and B, for whom $G_t^A = G_t^B$.

This principle states explicitly what several theories of language assume: no two individuals share the same version of the grammar of the language they speak and write at any one moment. This also implies that it is unlikely for two individuals to have the exact same idiolect at the end of their lives. That no two individuals are the same or, at least, that it is very unlikely to meet two identical linguistic individuals has been the most fundamental working assumption adopted by studies and casework on authorship analysis. However, as explained in Section 1.4, a substantial body of indirect evidence has been accrued such that it makes sense to consider this assumption a basic principle.

The main reason why each individual's grammar must be unique is that something that counts as a unit for one individual might not necessarily count as a unit for another individual. Although there is enough evidence to support this claim, what is far less known is the extent to which individuals share units. A *weak* form of the principle would mean that differences between individuals are minimal and just enough for them to be identified through the language they use, as demonstrated by research in authorship analysis. In contrast, a *strong* version of the principle could imply that our conception that all speakers of a language share most of its grammar is an illusion given by the fact that, although each individual's grammar is unique, these grammars are mutually understandable.

2.3.1 The Linguistic Fingerprint

The Principle of Linguistic Individuality therefore comes very close to arguing for a *linguistic fingerprint*. However, because an individual's grammar is constantly shaped by usage, the Principle of Linguistic Individuality makes it clear that this metaphor is only valid if we consider a specific time window, unlike actual fingerprints. The theory, however, does not specify exactly the length of this time window t. For the present work, it is only important that this insight is included in the theory, pending future research on the stability of an individual's mental grammars over time. Because we know that authorship analysis is possible, we do not expect this window to be very short, as analyses of historical data also suggest (Fonteyn, 2021).

Another objection to the notion of linguistic fingerprints apart from change over time has been their incommensurability. For example, Coulthard (2004, p. 432) argued that:

> the concept of the linguistic fingerprint is an unhelpful, if not actually misleading metaphor [...] because it leads us to imagine the creation of massive databanks consisting of representative linguistic samples (or summary analyses) of millions of idiolects [...] such an enterprise is, and for the

> foreseeable future will continue to be, impractical if not impossible [..] any
> linguistic sample, even a very large one, provides only very partial informa-
> tion about its creator's idiolect.

Similarly, Grant and MacLeod (2018, p. 83) wrote that 'it is clear that even vast quantities of linguistic data from many individuals could not fully substantiate Coulthard's strong assertion of linguistic uniqueness'.

Although the assumption of the impossibility of capturing an idiolect is plausible as an a priori position, this limitation can be challenged by this theory if we consider what we know about the mathematical laws of language. For example, the relationship between word tokens observed and new word types discovered is very well known in linguistics and goes by the name of *Herdan's law* (Herdan, 1960). The law can be described in the following manner:

$$V = N^\alpha$$

where V is the number of types in a corpus and N is the number of tokens in the same corpus and α is an exponent that depends on the data set but that is a positive number smaller than 1. This law is actually also known as *Heaps' law* because Heaps demonstrated that it applies to many other phenomena involving a relationship between *tokens* and *types* (Heaps, 1978). Assuming $\alpha = 0.7$, the equation can be graphed as in Figure 5.

A consequence of this law is that there are diminishing returns in how many types are discovered the more tokens are seen. For example, let's assume a scenario where we want to study the vocabulary of a person and we start collecting data from them in batches of 1,000 words. With $\alpha = 0.7$, then after 1,000 tokens are collected we expect to find 126 types that are repeated several times, meaning that 13% of the 1,000 tokens is the vocabulary we discovered.

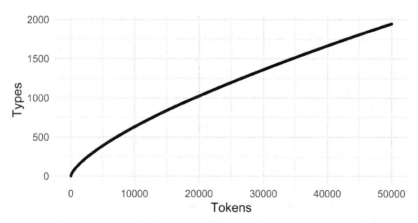

Figure 5 Herdan–Heaps' law with $\alpha = 0.7$.

Adding another 1,000 tokens means that we discover about 78 new types, bringing the number of total types to 204, which is, however, only 10% of the tokens. Thus, collecting more tokens leads to a decreasing number of new types being discovered proportionally speaking. In other words, the more tokens we add the lower the probability that we encounter new types. Once we are in the range of millions of tokens, the fraction of them that are different token types is only 1.6% and adding another 1,000 does not really make any difference. Although all this concerns the lexicon, in principle this relationship should apply to grammar as well, if we conceive of a grammar as a repository of units.

Herdan–Heaps' law does not have an upper boundary, meaning that no matter how many tokens one observes, the number of types will keep growing infinitely. This has been empirically demonstrated on very large corpora of language where increasing the number of tokens always leads to an increasing number of types. This result is however dependent on the fact that a token is defined as a sequence of characters in between spaces, which therefore includes typos or sequences such as *haha* that can be extended. In reality, there is a point of inflection after which the core vocabulary is exhausted and this core vocabulary is in the order of thousands or tens of thousands of units (Gerlach and Altmann, 2013). The expectation is that the same should be true for a G_t, where a set of units constitutes the core and this number is not so large as to become impractical.

Knowing that such a critical threshold exists, then the empirical question is: how much text does one need to observe to approximate the core grammar of a person, or at very least the core grammar for one register? Although we will not know the exact amount until we have some empirical verification with real data, mathematically and theoretically speaking this task is not as impossible as previously theorised. If Herdan–Heaps' law applies to G_t, then, although this is infinitely productive, it can still be described, exactly like the lexicon of a language.

2.4 The Statistical Approximation Hypothesis

Before moving on to the next two sections showing how the theory can be implemented in practice, this section establishes a link between the present theory and past work in authorship analysis.

As explained above, there is no good reason to explain why individuals manifest certain preferences for functors which make up the key profiles. For example, saying that an author uses *the* 12.3% of the times they write a word is meaningless because, firstly, this item does not necessarily constitute a choice in itself and, secondly, it cannot just be due to preference. However, linguistic units as defined in this theory can and indeed often are themselves made up of functors such as *the* and therefore a connection between this theory and the frequency methods can be established. This connection is formulated as the *Statistical Approximation Hypothesis*:

> The *Statistical Approximation Hypothesis*: an author's Key Profile is a statistical representation approximating their G_t.

The hypothesis is essentially stating that frequency of functors identifies authors because it implicitly contains information about their G_t. For example, consider these two toy grammars from two hypothetical individuals, A and B, sampled from texts they produced within the same time window:[4]

$$G_t^A = \{[\text{V N} \text{ on the } \text{N}], [rather\ than], [give\ \text{N}\ to\ \text{N}], [half\ \text{N}], [help\ \text{V}],$$
$$[try\ to\ \text{V}], [sort\ of]\}$$

$$G_t^B = \{[\text{V N} \text{ with } \text{N}], [instead\ of], [give\ \text{N N}], [half\ of\ \text{N}], [help\ to\ \text{V}],$$
$$[try\ and\ \text{V}], [kind\ of]\}$$

If we then analyse two texts written by these two individuals, T_t^A and T_t^B, where each unit appears only once, we can compile the matrix of word counts in Table 3.

This matrix of word token counts traditionally used for authorship analysis, especially when only considering function words or other functors, could therefore be a statistical representation of the units in the author's grammar. This hypothesis effectively explains why frequency of word tokens or short character n-grams work: each unit contains a different configuration of function words and morphemes and, if people's inventories of units are different, then this will also result in different profiles of frequencies of function words and morphemes because the frequency with which a word occurs reflects an individual's selection of units.

This hypothesis makes verifiable predictions. If the hypothesis is correct, then methods that better reflect this Theory of Linguistic Individuality should perform at least equally well or outperform methods based on frequencies, which are instead just approximations to the first. The rest of this Element will address this prediction and show how the theory can be translated into a methodology to analyse and compare texts for the purposes of authorship analysis.

3 Applying the Theory to Authorship Analysis

Following the present theory, authorship analysis can be thought of as the process of expressing the likelihood that a particular $\hat{G}_t$ extracted from texts produced by a suspect is the same $\hat{G}_t$ that produced the disputed text T_Q.

---

[4] The examples are taken from Nini *et al.* (2021).

Table 3 Sample of word token count matrix from toy texts written by two individuals.

	on	the	rather	than	give	to	half	help	try	sort	of	with	instead	and	kind
T_t^A	1	1	1	1	1	2	1	1	1	1	1	0	0	0	0
T_t^B	0	0	0	0	1	1	1	1	1	0	3	1	1	1	1

Authorship analysis is therefore conceptually very similar to partial finger-print matching: in a text we can find a subset of a G_t in the same way that a partial fingerprint contains a subset of minutiae of a full fingerprint. The identification consists in the assessment of the similarities and the extent to which these are due to chance or to them being produced by the same unique G_t.

If we think of authorship analysis in this way, then two components are needed to carry it out:

1. A *grammar induction function*, as defined in Section 2.2.5, that takes as input one or more texts T and returns as output a grammar $\hat{G}_t$, which is likely to be an approximation to the real grammar G_t.
2. A *measure* or *algorithm* to quantify the match between the various candidate authors' extracted grammars, $\hat{G}_t^A, \hat{G}_t^B, \hat{G}_t^C \ldots \hat{G}_t^N$, and the extracted grammar of the questioned text, $\hat{G}_t^Q$.

3.1 Grammar Induction

Theoretically, there are many ways to extract a grammatical representation from a text or corpus, with varying degrees of cognitive realism. The best function, in particular for the purposes of authorship analysis, can only be found through many empirical studies.

The most basic and yet cognitively plausible way to extract a grammar from a corpus is to use n-grams. These representations are more cognitively realis-tic than simple words (see Section 1.3.2). In computational linguistics, the first pioneering language models were indeed created using n-grams before even-tually becoming more sophisticated through the use of neural networks, making them more effective but less amenable to interpretation (Jurafsky and Martin, 2009). Training a neural network on a corpus could be a way to arrive at a $\hat{G}_t$ too but for the purposes of forensic linguistics the lack of transparency is an issue.

Although somewhat acceptable, n-grams are generally unsatisfactory as a representation of grammar because they do not capture sophisticated abstractions or units that are not sequential. For example, word n-grams fail to recognise word forms that belong to the same lemma. Although this could be fixed by using a part-of-speech tagger, it is clearly a less than ideal solution. In addition, any n-gram requires the decision as to what n to use. The ideal grammar induction function should contain as few arbitrary decisions as possible by including knowledge from cognitive science to guide the decisions.

An example of a middle ground between just n-grams and more complex representations is Dunn's (2017) algorithm to automatically extract a construction grammar given a corpus. This algorithm considers various levels of abstraction at the same time, thus returning units that mix words, lemmas, parts of speech, and semantic tags so long as they meet a collocation statistic threshold.

Despite promising advances, at this point in time there are no ready solutions to this problem and, even if there were, it would still be useful to establish a benchmark using the simplest possible method. In this work, therefore, the grammatical induction function is simply the extraction of n-grams. A grammar induction function based on n-grams needs at the very least three parameters to be set: (1) the level of abstraction of the n-gram; (2) the n; and (3) the value of frequency to promote a token to unit.

Four levels of abstraction are considered: character n-grams, word n-grams, part-of-speech (POS) n-grams, and *frame* n-grams. The last type is a novel way to extract n-grams at a medium level of abstraction, similar to Wible and Tsao's (2010) *hybrid n-grams*, Sinclair's *collocational frame-works* (Renouf and Sinclair, 1991), or the patterns of *Pattern Grammar* (Hunston and Francis, 2000). These frame n-grams are created by first tagging the data using a POS tagger and then keeping only the tags for nouns, personal pronouns, and verbs, which are the most likely categories to contain content information, and keeping only the word forms for other parts of speech. Table 4 shows examples of 3-grams of these four types using the same short phrase.

As demonstrated in this table, punctuation marks are always retained as if they were a word token.

Due to the explorational nature of the present work, it is useful to include as many values of n as possible. For this reason, the lengths considered are: $2 \leq n \leq 9$ for character n-grams, $1 \leq n \leq 8$ for word n-grams, and $1 \leq n \leq 10$ for both POS n-grams and frame n-grams.

Finally, a minimum frequency could be set in order to decide what n-grams to include in the $\hat{G}_t$ and what to exclude as potential noise. For instance, an n-gram like 'golden_bands_,' could occur only once in a text and one way to proceed would be to exclude it because there is not enough evidence that this is a unit for the individual who produced it. Thus, one could set the minimum frequency to > 1 to avoid this potential confounding factor. For the experiments illustrated below, however, no minimum frequency was chosen. Any n-gram found even only once was included in the final set representing the $\hat{G}_t$.

Table 4 Examples of the types of n-grams used. Each n-gram is contained in double quotes.

Plain text	Word 3-grams	Character 3-grams	POS 3-grams	Frames 3-grams
lay in broad, golden bands, upon the flags of the convent cloister	"lay_in_broad_" "in_broad_,_golden" "broad_,_golden" ",_golden_bands" "golden_bands_,_" "bands_,_upon" ",_upon_the" "upon_the_flags" "the_flags_of" "flags_of_the" "of_the_convent" "the_convent_cloister"	"lay" "ay " "y i" "i " "in" "in " "n b" "br" "bro" "roa" "oad" "ad," "d, " "g" " go" "gol" "old" "lde" "den" "en " "n b" "ba" "ban" "and" "nds" "ds," "s, " ", u" " up" "upo" "pon" "on " "n t" " th" "the" "he " "e f" "fl" "fla" "lag" "ags" "gs " "s o" "of " "of " "f t" " th" "the" "he " "e c" "co" "con" "onv" "nve" "ven" "ent" "nt" "t c" "cl" "clo" "loi" "ois" "ist" "ste" "ter" "er."	"vbd_in_jj" "in_jj " "in_jj ,_" "jj ,_jj_" "jj" ",_jj_nns" "jj_nns_," "nns_,_in" ",_in_dt" "in_dt_nns" "dt_nns_in" "nns_in_dt" "in_dt_nnp" "dt_nnp_nm"	"vbd_in_broad" "in_broad_," "broad_,_golden" ",_golden_nns" "golden_nns_," "nns_,_upon" ",_upon_the" "upon_the_nns" "the_nns_of" "nns_of_the" "of_the_nnp" "the_nnp_nm"

3.2 Measures of Similarity

Once a grammar induction function has been applied to a text, a set of units is produced, which is what we call $\hat{G}_t$. As explained in Section 2.2.2, although the best representation for a grammar is as a network, for simplicity a set of units is used instead. The question of comparing grammars therefore boils down to how to measure the similarity between sets. From a purely mathematical perspective, there are many ways to compare sets. To find the right way, one can select the best methods either theoretically or empirically via testing, which is the approach taken in this work.

In its most basic sense, measuring the amount of similarity between two sets of items could simply mean quantifying the overlap, as in Figure 4. That overlap, $G^A \cap G^B$, contains the following units:

$$G^A \cap G^B = \{[dog], [hope], [the\ N\ of]\}$$

An alternative mathematical representation of the two overlapping sets embedded in a language L_t in Figure 4 can be obtained by using *binary vectors*. Similarly to the numeric vectors explained in Section 1.2.1, a binary vector is a vector that can contain only 0 (a feature is absent) or 1 (a feature is present), as in Table 5.

Table 5 shows more clearly how the two grammars can also have in common the *absence* of certain units which, however, exist in L_t. An important methodological decision is therefore whether common absences should be counted or not.

Even if we decided to only focus on the common presences, just counting the items in the overlap is not the only way or the best way possible to quantify similarity. In fact, the most common way of measuring the similarity of binary vectors of this kind is the Jaccard coefficient, initially introduced as a way to measure similarities in ecology in Jaccard (1912). This coefficient is calculated using the following formula, where the vertical bars indicate the cardinality of the set; that is, the number of items it contains:

$$J_{(G_t^A, G_t^B)} = \frac{|G_t^A \cap G_t^B|}{|G_t^A \cup G_t^B|}.$$

In other words, the Jaccard coefficient is the ratio between the overlap and the union of two sets. For the example in Table 5, the overlap would be the third column, where a 1 marks the elements that appear in both sets. The union, instead, would be the sum of all the units that appear in either one of the grammars, so the sum of all the 1s. The Jaccard coefficient for the example in Table 5 is therefore $\frac{3}{8} = 0.375$. The Jaccard coefficient is one of the most

Table 5 Representation of Figure 4 using binary vectors.

Units	G_t^A	G_t^B	$G_t^A \cap G_t^B$
[*arguably*]	0	0	0
[*technician*]	0	0	0
[N V N P N]	0	0	0
[*although*]	1	0	0
[*-ness*]	1	0	0
[*respectfully*]	1	0	0
[N V P]	1	0	0
[*dog*]	1	1	1
[*hope*]	1	1	1
[*the* N *of*]	1	1	1
[*However,*]	0	0	0
[*can* V A V]	0	1	0

common ways to measure similarities between two binary vectors because when dividing the overlap by the union one is effectively putting both sets on to the same playing field: when using the Jaccard coefficient the elements that are present in the universe outside of the two sets being compared (in our case L_t), are not considered.

The Jaccard coefficient has already been used in forensic linguistics. Originally introduced in the field by Grant (2010) as a way to measure similarity between text messages, it was later adopted for various other studies in forensic authorship analysis, such as Wright (2013, 2017) and Nini (2018). The Jaccard coefficient was initially adopted by Grant (2010) precisely because it does not count common absences. The argument is that this is a desirable property when dealing with text messages because these texts are short and therefore the absence of a feature does not automatically mean that that feature is absent in the grammar of the author.

Although Grant's (2010) assumption is plausible, the question of including or excluding common absences in binary vector comparison is not at all straightforward and it has been widely discussed, for example in biology and ecology (Hayek, 1994; Warrens, 2008, p. 5). To resolve this issue, the approach taken in this work is to carry out a survey of all possible binary coefficients, like Jaccard, and then test empirically which one is the most suitable. For this reason, a set of 22 coefficients is considered. Before presenting the list of coefficients, however, it is necessary to introduce the terminology used to describe them.

Let us imagine two sets such as the ones in Figure 6, which is a more general abstract representation of the linguistic example shown in Figure 4.

Figure 6 shows the quantities that are commonly considered when calculating binary coefficients in both graphical representation and set notation. The figure shows a universe of features U with two sets, A and B, and their intersection. Each quadrant of the features represents a quantity that can be calculated from this setting and that is indicated by a letter in small capitals:

- The number of elements in the intersection, $|A \cap B|$, is commonly indicated with a.
- The letters b and c respectively indicate the number of elements that only belong to one of the two sets and that are not shared with the other.
- The letter d indicates everything else in the universe of features that is not in either of the two sets. This can be indicated as in Figure 6 as $|\overline{A \cup B}|$, or alternatively, as the number of elements in the universe minus the union of A and B, thus $|U| - |A \cup B|$.
- Finally, the letter p, not in the picture, usually indicates the sum of all the quantities above, so $p = a + b + c + d$.

This notation is far more convenient because, for example, we can now rewrite the Jaccard coefficient as:

$$J_{(G_t^A, G_t^B)} = \frac{a}{a + b + c}.$$

This way of representing similarity coefficients for binary data is more economical and will be implemented throughout the rest of the work.

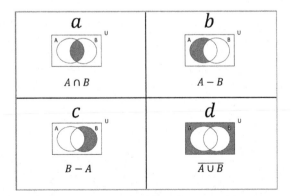

Figure 6 Example of intersection between two sets, A and B, in a universe of features U.

The coefficients explored in this work were taken from the comprehensive survey of 51 binary coefficients carried out by Todeschini *et al.* (2012). The analysis of their correlations found that 28 out of 51 were either perfectly or highly correlated with other coefficients in terms of the relative ranking that they produce. Because the use of these coefficients in this work is mostly about producing a rank, highly correlated coefficients can be safely excluded from further consideration. The analyses in the present work are therefore carried out using the coefficients listed in Table 6.

Table 6 List of coefficients considered in the present work. The table lists the name of the coefficient, the formula, the key references in which it was proposed, and its class.

Name	Formula	References	Class
Simple Matching	$\dfrac{a+d}{p}$	Sokal and Michener (1958)	symmetric
Jaccard	$\dfrac{a}{a+b+c}$	Jaccard (1912)	asymmetric
Russell–Rao	$\dfrac{a}{p}$	Russell and Rao (1940)	asymmetric
Simpson	$\dfrac{a}{\min((a+b),(a+c))}$	Simpson (1943)	asymmetric
Braun-Blanquet	$\dfrac{a}{\max((a+b),(a+c))}$	Braun-Blanquet (1932)	asymmetric
Ochiai	$\dfrac{a}{\sqrt{(a+b)(a+c)}}$	Driver and Kroeber (1932) Ochiai (1957)	asymmetric
Kulczynski	$\dfrac{1}{2}\left(\dfrac{a}{a+b}+\dfrac{a}{a+c}\right)$	Kulczynski (1927)	asymmetric
Mountford	$\dfrac{2a}{ab+ac+2bc}$	Mountford (1962)	asymmetric
Rogot–Goldberg	$\dfrac{a}{2a+b+c}+\dfrac{d}{2d+b+c}$	Rogot and Goldberg (1966)	symmetric
Hawkins–Dotson	$\dfrac{1}{2}\left(\dfrac{a}{a+b+c}+\dfrac{d}{d+b+c}\right)$	Hawkins and Dotson (1968)	symmetric
Yule	$\dfrac{\sqrt{ad}-\sqrt{bc}}{\sqrt{ad}+\sqrt{bc}}$	Yule (1900, 1912)	correlation
Cole	$\dfrac{ad-bc}{(a+c)(c+d)}$	Cole (1949)	correlation
Goodman– Kruskal	$\dfrac{2\min(a,d)-b-c}{2\min(a,d)+b+c}$	Goodman and Kruskal (1954)	symmetric
Sokal–Sneath	$\dfrac{a}{\sqrt{(a+b)(a+c)}}\dfrac{d}{\sqrt{(d+b)(d+c)}}$	Sokal and Sneath (1963)	symmetric

Table 6 (cont.)

Name	Formula	References	Class
Phi	$\dfrac{ad - bc}{\sqrt{(a+b)(a+c)(c+d)(b+d)}}$	Pearson and Heron (1913)	correlation
Sorgenfrei	$\dfrac{a^2}{(a+b)(a+c)}$	Sorgenfrei (1958)	asymmetric
Cohen	$\dfrac{2(ad - bc)}{(a+b)(b+d) + (a+c)(c+d)}$	Cohen (1960)	correlation
Consonni–Todeschini 3	$\dfrac{\ln(1+a)}{\ln(1+p)}$	Consonni and Todeschini (2012)	asymmetric
Consonni–Todeschini 5	$\dfrac{\ln(1+ad) - \ln(1+bc)}{\ln\left(1 + \frac{p^2}{4}\right)}$	Consonni and Todeschini (2012)	symmetric

The list also contains information about the *class* of the coefficient.[5] The main difference is whether a coefficient contains the quantity d or not, meaning whether the coefficient counts common absences, or *negative matches*, or only common presences, or *positive matches*. Todeschini *et al.* (2012) classify as *symmetric* those coefficients that equally weight positive and negative matches, while the *asymmetric* coefficients are those that only consider positive matches. All the coefficients are similarity (or distance) coefficients, like Delta. Their value ranges from 1, if the two sets are identical, to 0, if the two sets are completely different. The only exceptions are the ones in the *correlation* class, which instead output a value between -1 and 1 representing the level of correlation between the two binary vectors considered. These correlation coefficients can also be mathematically transformed so that their output is bounded between 0 and 1.

Table 6 shows the variety of possibilities that are available to quantify the similarity between two sets, which demonstrates in principle that it is not immediately obvious how one would choose the way to proceed to measure similarity of binary vectors for authorship analysis. This question is addressed empirically in the rest of this section, where the coefficients above are compared to each other and to Delta.

---

[5] Todeschini *et al.* (2012) also include the *intermediate* class, in which coefficients count negative matches but they do not weight them equally to positive matches. Because this class only contains two coefficients and these were found to perform poorly in initial testing, this class is excluded entirely for simplicity. Similarly, the two *Cole* coefficients are reduced to only one because initial testing shows they are highly correlated.

3.3 A Reinterpretation of the N-gram Tracing Method

Besides the Jaccard coefficient as implemented by Johnson and Wright (2014) and Wright (2017), another authorship analysis method that uses a binary coefficient to compare sets is the *n-gram tracing* method introduced by Grieve *et al.* (2019), which is also quite similar to Coulthard's (2013) method.

The n-gram tracing algorithm is the following:

1. Take the disputed text (Q) and break it down into n-grams (e.g. of characters or words) of a length n.
2. For each text belonging to the candidate authors:
   a. Take the candidate author's text and break it down into the same n-gram type and length as done for Q so as to create a set of n-grams for each candidate's text.
   b. Take the union of all the candidate's sets of n-grams.
3. Attribute the Q text to the candidate whose n-gram set shares the highest percentage of n-gram types with Q.

The method can be represented using the following formula:

$$S_{(Q,A)} = \frac{|Q \cap \bigcup_i T_i^A|}{|Q|}.$$

where Q is the set of n-grams in the Q text, T_i^A is the set of n-grams extracted from the text T_i of the set of texts written by author A, $A = \{T_1, T_2, T_3, \dots T_n\}$, and thus $\bigcup T_i^A$ is the union of all these sets of n-grams. The resulting $S_{(Q,A)}$ is the similarity coefficient that represents how much of Q is in A. Because it is assumed that in all cases $|Q| \ll |\bigcup T_i^A|$, which is a realistic assumption in forensic contexts, then the formula above is essentially the same as the one for the *overlap* or *Simpson's coefficient* (see Table 6).

The formula above can be easily adapted to the theory by substituting Q with $\hat{G}_t^Q$, the grammar extracted from the disputed texts, and $\bigcup T_i^A$ with $\hat{G}_t^A$, the grammar extracted from the texts collected for the candidate. Thus,

$$S_{(Q,A)} = \frac{|\hat{G}_t^Q \cap \hat{G}_t^A|}{|\hat{G}_t^Q|}.$$

For example, let us assume we have one disputed text, Q, and we break it down into the set of its constituting n-grams, $\hat{G}_t^Q = \{[respectfully], [can\ V\ A\ V], [although], [dog]\}$. The number of items in this set is $|\hat{G}_t^Q| = 4$. Looking back at Table 5, we can now calculate $S_{(Q,A)}$ for candidates A and B.

$$S_{(Q,A)} = \frac{|\hat{G}_t^Q \cap \hat{G}_t^A|}{|\hat{G}_t^Q|} = \frac{3}{4} = 0.75$$

$$S_{(Q,B)} = \frac{|\hat{G}_t^Q \cap \hat{G}_t^B|}{|\hat{G}_t^Q|} = \frac{2}{4} = 0.5$$

Because the score for A is higher, then A is more likely to be the author of Q than B.

The example above shows the comparison of two grammars represented as sets of units using n-gram tracing, or the Simpson coefficient. The three experiments in this section are fundamentally based on the same procedure but use the array of coefficients seen in Table 6 to compare the performance to the benchmark of Delta.

3.4 Experiment 1: The *refcor* Corpus

The first computational experiment reported in this work is a comparison between Delta and the method described in Section 3.3 based on the present theory. The aim of this experiment is twofold: (1) to test whether this method works as well as or better than Delta, and thus whether there is support for the Statistical Approximation Hypothesis; (2) to test which ones among the binary coefficients and the features are better for identification to substantiate the validity of the theoretical claims made above. Providing the answers to these research questions can inform the pursuit of an application of the present theory to authorship analysis.

This first experiment uses the English section of the *refcor* corpus of literary works (Jannidis *et al.*, 2015; Evert *et al.*, 2017).[6] This section of the corpus contains texts collected from Project Gutenberg – more precisely, 75 novels from 25 authors with each author contributing 3 novels. Although texts of this kind are not particularly forensically realistic, novels from famous authors have the advantage of containing a lot of data, which is a requirement to experiment with various parameters.

As a benchmark to evaluate performance, the binary coefficients listed in Table 6 are compared to the best Delta coefficient types tested by Evert *et al.* (2017): Cosine Delta and Cosine Delta with Evert's modification, from now on called *Evert's Delta*. In contrast to Evert *et al.* (2017), however, the present experiment does not measure performance using a clustering technique but by using the *k-nearest neighbours* algorithm with $k = 1$, as most commonly done

---

[6] https://github.com/cophi-wue/refcor.

for analyses using Delta. In simple words, this means that the candidates are ranked from most similar to most dissimilar to the questioned text and the most similar candidate is assigned as the author of the questioned text. The algorithm adopted for this experiment was the following:

(1) For each Q length: 50, 100, 300, 500, 1000, 2000, 5000.
(2) For each K length: 2,000, 5,000, 10,000, 20,000, 50,000, 100,000, 130,000.
(3) For each text in the *refcor* corpus:
   (a) the text was removed and labelled as the Q text;
   (b) a random sample of the Q texts of size equal to one of the lengths in (1) was taken;
   (c) the remaining texts in the corpus were combined by author to form one large sample for each author;
   (d) a random sample was taken from each author's corpus equal to one of the lengths in (2);
   (e) the Q random sample and the authors' samples were recombined into one data set;
   (f) this data set was broken down into n-grams as shown in Table 4;
   (g) the coefficients in Table 6 were calculated. In addition, Cosine Delta and Evert's Delta were also calculated to be used as benchmarks. For these, only the 3,000 most frequent features in the corpus were considered (Evert *et al.*, 2017);
   (h) the rank of the correct author was determined. If there was a tie, then the *max* method was used, meaning that both authors received the lowest rank (e.g. if author A and author B are both tied in first position, they both receive the second position). This is the most conservative way to calculate a rank so that if the correct author is tied with someone else this is still considered a failed test.

The cycle above was repeated five times to mitigate the effect of chance, which means that for each text in *refcor* five random samples for each sample size were extracted and the results discussed below are the average values of these five repetitions.

Figure 7 is a visual representation as a heatmap of the performance of the coefficients and of the features. Each cell of the matrix represents the median rank of the correct author for that combination of coefficient and feature. Darker shades indicate lower ranks, meaning that the darker the cell is, the better the performance of that combination. To aid interpretation, both rows and columns were sorted by rank so that the combinations of features and coefficients close to the bottom left corner are the ones that best perform overall.

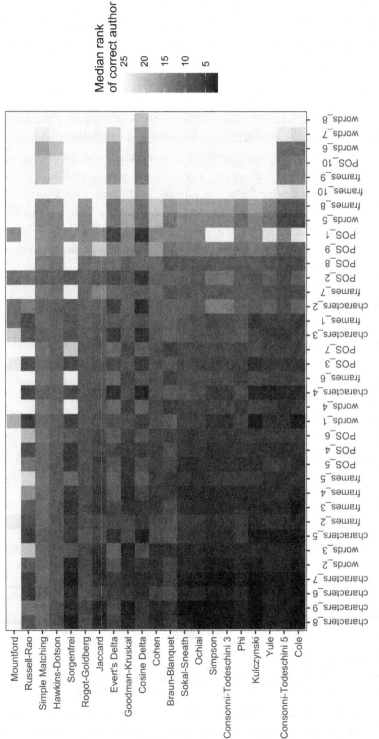

Figure 7 Heatmap visualising the matrix with each coefficient as rows and each feature as columns. The cells are the median rank for each combination of coefficient and feature. The order of the rows and columns is given by the rank.

Several facts about the coefficients are evident from this graph. Firstly, coefficients at the top of the matrix such as Mountford, Russell–Rao, or Simple Matching do not perform well, no matter what feature is used. In contrast, the best coefficients are Cole, Consonni-Todeschini 5, Yule, Kulczynski, and Phi. The Simpson coefficient, which is essentially n-gram tracing, performs well but not as well as these other coefficients. Three of these coefficients contain information about negative matches because they are either symmetrical or correlational coefficients, which is very surprising given the small sizes of Q considered. The Delta coefficients do not perform as well as one would expect given previous studies but it is evident that Cosine Delta is a valuable coefficient if used with the right features, character 4-grams, 3-grams, or 2-grams, or POS 1-grams or 2-grams. Another interesting point to make is that Jaccard does not perform very well overall. As for the features, the evidence points to the best ones being long character n-grams, in particular n = 8 to n = 9, followed by word n-grams, n = 2 to n = 3, then frames with n = 2 to n = 3, and finally POS with n = 4 to n = 5.

Figure 8 shows the relationship between the accuracy of the identification, in the form of median rank, and the feature types. The value on the vertical axis is the median rank achieved by each feature (only considering the best coefficients: Cole, Consonni-Todeschini 5, Kulczynski, Phi, and Yule) while the horizontal axis shows the increasing length of the sample for the author, while each section of the graph represents the values for a size of Q.

The figure suggests that even though the correct author might not be always the most similar one to Q, it is very often at least in the top half of the ranking, out of 25 possible positions.

The figure also makes very clear that the best feature is overwhelmingly character 9-grams, almost always followed by word 2-grams, and then frame 3-grams and POS 5-grams. Despite their lower performance, the last two are still valid features, especially when the length of the texts becomes larger and the gap between the feature types becomes small. This pattern means that the feature type becomes less important when a lot of comparison data is available. For the strictest test of a Q text of 50 tokens, the results suggest that it is possible to narrow down the correct author within the top three using character 9-grams only when 130,000 token known samples are available. However, even for texts as short as 50 tokens, it is still possible with any feature type to narrow down the search to the top half of a list of 25 authors. Performance then improves as Q and K samples become longer, as expected, until reaching the median rank of 1 for character 9-grams when the Q text is 300 tokens and the

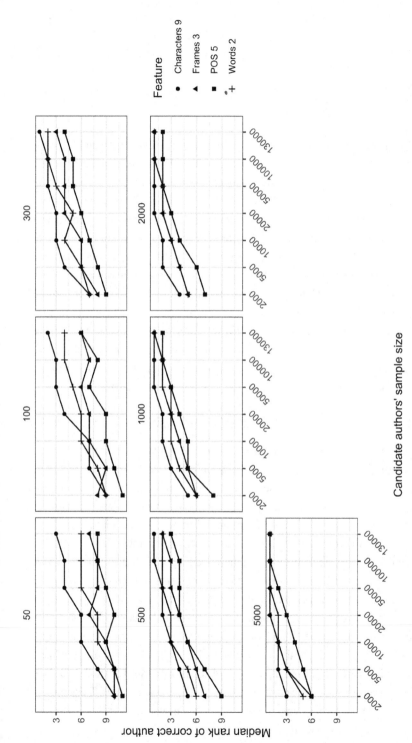

Figure 8 Chart showing the median rank of the correct author depending on the length of the Q text and the length of the authors' samples for the best feature of each type.

known samples are 130,000 tokens. When the Q text is 2,000 or 5,000 tokens, then known samples of 20,000 tokens are sufficient to obtain a correct attribution.

Figure 9 shows the performance of the coefficients. This figure should be read in the same way as Figure 8, the difference being that the dots represent the top-performing coefficients plus Cosine Delta and Simpson (n-gram tracing), which are added for comparison.

The most evident pattern is the gap between Cosine Delta and the other coefficients when short Q texts are considered, with Cosine Delta being considerably outperformed. The only setting in which Cosine Delta is comparable to the binary coefficients is when the Q text is 5,000 words and this is compatible with previous results (Proisl *et al.*, 2018). In contrast, the remaining binary coefficients are all pretty much equal in performance. The only other pattern to note is that Cole seems to be even better than others when Q is very short. It seems therefore that Cole should be considered the best coefficient overall because it performs well for both short and long Q texts. It is crucial to note that Cole is a correlational coefficient that includes information about common absences and the fact that such a coefficient work very well even for short Q texts means that ignoring common absences leads to a loss of information. In conclusion, the results confirm that the binary coefficients work as well if not better than Delta and that the best coefficients are the ones that count negative matches.

3.4.1 Individuality in n-grams

An objection to the use of presence/absence of n-grams is that the method is picking up on extremely rare and perhaps topical features. Although this cannot be the case for POS and frame n-grams, this could explain the much better performance of character and word n-grams. To verify this and increase our understanding, a sample of word 2-grams and frame 3-grams that are used only by one author across at least two texts are displayed in Table 7.

Table 7 shows that relatively few of these seemingly idiolectal units are dependent on topic or can be explained by factors other than the Principle of Linguistic Individuality. Thackeray's [*at lambeth*] is potentially a confounding 2-gram and so is Doyle's [*holmes.*]. However, most of the n-grams in the table, like Thackeray's [*affectionate old*], can only be explained by the present theory. It is also quite intriguing how several of these unique word 2-grams do not look particularly exotic or idiosyncratic, for example Meredith's [*disarmed him*] or Doyle's [*starting upon*]. The problem of topic or names is resolved by frame 3-grams. There are very interesting idiolectal n-grams in the list that again would otherwise seem quite common, such as [VBG *desperately,*], [*ashore with* PRP], [*nevertheless* VBD

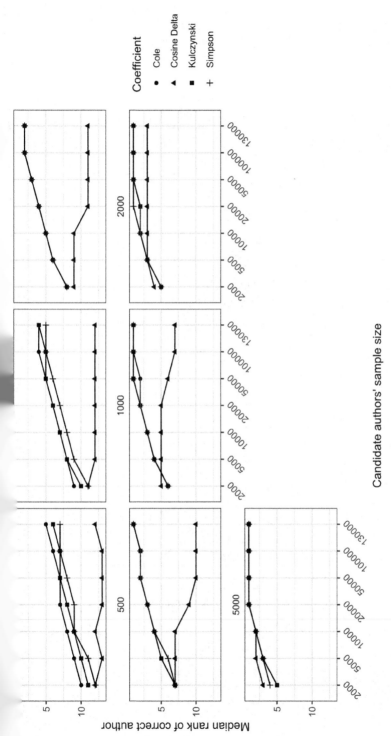

Figure 9 Graph showing the median rank of the correct author achieved as a function of the length of the candidate authors' samples and the size of the Q text for some of the top performing coefficients (Cole, Kulczynski,) plus Cosine Delta and Simpson.

Table 7 A random sample of, respectively, three word 2-grams, three frame 3-grams, and three character 9-grams for each author. Each n-gram is used only by that author in at least two of their texts.

Author	n-grams
Barclay	softly_moving|stately_grace|felt_constrained
	softly_vbg_nns|;_and_together|silently_,_vbd
	oftly mov|. all nat|aiting ar
Blackmore	by_perpetual|thinking_twice|furlong_,
	by_perpetual_nn|vbg_yet_to|steadfast_,_and
	dfully ho| sting-ne|sting-net
Braddon	quadrangle_.|liverpool_in|coquettish_little
	purple_nns_vbp|good_nns_once|nn_vb_calm
	adrangle.|drangle. |m life is
Burnett	ill_himself|hot_morning|the_ayah
	next_nn_three|prp_thin_little|queerer_than_ever
	d flew aw|m and sla|ched quit
C. Bronte	a_preternatural|door_unclosed|rather_young
	a_preternatural_nn|the_solitary_and|the_nn_unclosed
	won't i| warm; th| becloude
Chesterton	is_founded|steep_streets|snail_,
	a_criminal_.|nn_the_short|nn_placidly_,
	antic ges| ntic gest| o kill.
Collins	interval_passed|and_discovering|my_anxieties
	honestly_vb_,|vbd_an_impenetrable|in_the_bygone
	rds, i ha|rval pass|val passe
Corelli	queried_,|of_olden|all_worlds
	vbp_vbn_nowadays|of_olden_nns|nns_of_creative
	queried,|queried, |ueried, w
Dickens	holborn_hill|file_and|beadle_,
	ashy_nn_.|a_n't_prp|but_once_and
	holborn h|olborn hi|lborn hil

Table 7 (cont.)

Author	n-grams
Doyle	starting_upon|mortimer_is|holmes_.
	vbg_desperately_,|hard_and_clear|of_this_unknown
	r such we|erous pap|rous pape
Eliot	the_bushy|no_blush|black_band
	the_bushy_nns|so_happy_now|too_strongly_on
	the bushy|he bushy | er's legs
Forster	of_tuscany|amenities_,|edged_round
	go_-_as|as_-_you|all_right_about
	of tusca|of tuscan|f tuscany
Gaskell	wife_lived|discordant_to|servant_)
	prp_vbd_na|na_vb_prp|vbd_too_indifferent
	h, had an|i'd ha' g|'d ha' gi
Gissing	become_self|in_kennington|her_expense
	nn_of_congenial|of_nn_suitable|too_much_alone
	ecome sel|come self| in kenni
Haggard	the_zulu|in_zululand|at_durban
	for_doubtless_prp|,_some_seventy|prp_spear_-
	the zulu|the zulu | in zulul
Hardy	woollen_cravat|'_hoi|twould_have
	vb_ee_to|ee_to_vb|nn_for_ee
	th wessex|e rectang| mellstoc
James	immediately_perceived|than_late|characteristically_,
	nevertheless_vbd_that|why_then_vb|'_vbz_magnificent '
	categorie|ategories|akes of i
Kipling	._d'you|huh_!|ulster_.
	blue_-_white|-_faring_nns|'_a_white
	. ho! ho!|s. he sli| oddments
Lytton	that_itinerant|he_prudently|from_sunrise
	vbp_a_keen|nn_,_admiringly|prp_prudently_vbd

Table 7 (cont.)

Author	n-grams
	ghly acco|ary estat| till doo
	chums_,|disarmed_him|shrugged_.
Meredith	nn_nnp_among|'_s_erratic|vbd_unacquainted_with
	she tole|she toler|ived peop
	sheer_rocks|somewhat_anigh|anigh_to
Morris ·	either_nn_thereof|of_diverse_nns|few_-_spoken
	whiles ca|hiles car|ewhat, th
	merry_word|fell_instantly|ashore_with
Stevenson	ashore_with_prp|and_the_dry|that_vbz_shall
	. thence,| in treas|and pipin
	few_scores|at_lambeth|affectionate_old
Thackeray	affectionate_old_nn|resolute_old_nn|vb_deservedly_vbn
	ew scores|w scores | mr. warr
	irish_members|far_between|still_doubted
Trollope	would_sooner_that|sooner_that_prp|no_;_-
	ew how gr|; – dear |' 'no; -
	party_they|stiffly_erect|restrain_.
Ward	ll_vb_home|bent_forward_eagerly|forward_eagerly_.
	ce she ra| book mar|dear – do

that], or [honestly VB,]. Character 9-grams are harder to interpret but overall they look like they are capturing word 2-grams while ignoring word boundaries, which allows them to capture approximations to units that are possibly more cognitively realistic, as the word boundary is artificial. In sum, the results lend support to the theory of individuality proposed in this work and, most importantly, to its foundation in usage-based cognitive linguistics.

3.4.2 Maximising Known Sample Length

The maximum known sample limit of 130,000 was chosen as this is the amount of data available for the author with the least amount of data. However, considering the above finding that an increase of the sample sizes leads to better performance, it would be interesting to find out what happens when much larger samples are considered, such as for the twelve authors in the corpus that have at least 300,000 tokens of data.

The same experiment was therefore carried out but this time keeping the known sample length constant at 300,000 tokens and varying only the length of Q and the features and coefficients. The only drawback of this follow-up experiment is the number of candidate authors is reduced by half and it is therefore more likely that the correct author is identified by chance.

The results are presented in Figure 10 and Figure 11, which respectively show the percentage of times that the correct author is found to be the most similar to Q or within the top three most similar authors to Q.

All results are greater than the chance baseline (8% and 25%). The figures show that, for Q texts as short as 50 tokens, more than 40% of the time the correct author is the top one out of twelve and in more than 60% of the time it is one of the top three. This performance increases gradually until it reaches close to 100% for Q texts with 5,000 tokens. Comparing the results of the binary coefficients to the performance of Cosine Delta, the latter only improves with the increase in Q size and for short Qs it remains around or just above baseline chance.

The results remain unchanged in terms of which feature is best (character 9-grams and word 2-grams) and show that, at this size, the coefficients that still perform well are only Cole, Kulczynski, and Simpson.

Although these results could suggest that adding more data to the known samples improves the results, the much smaller pool of authors could also be responsible for this improvement. For this reason, Figure 12 plots the performance for these same 12 authors using 150,000 token samples vs 300,000 token samples, only using the Simpson coefficient.

The graph shows that in most cases adding 150,000 tokens does not really justify the improvement obtained. This conclusion seems to be in line with what has been proposed in Section 2.3.1 regarding the effect of the Herdan–Heaps' law on the collection of an individual's full grammar.

3.5 Experiment 2: The *c50* Corpus

The first experiment and its follow-ups have been carried out on a corpus that is realistic for literary applications of authorship analysis but unusual for forensic linguistics. In addition, because the English *refcor* is made up of texts that are not synchronic, a possible objection could be that the findings do not generalise to modern texts. Apart from this limitation, there is also a problem of replicability. Outside of some natural sciences, it is unlikely that a single experiment can find

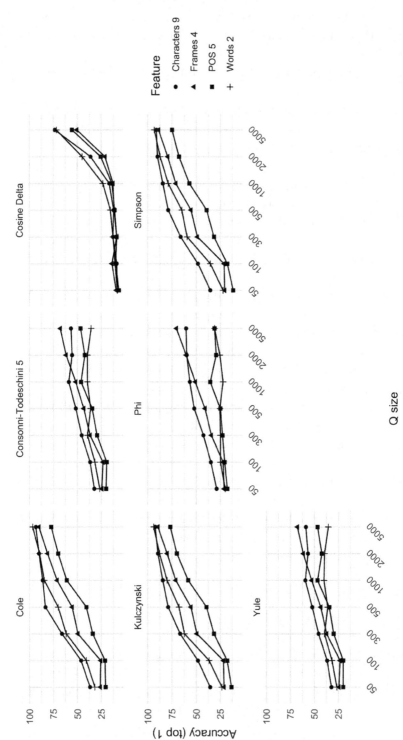

Figure 10 Percentage of times that the correct author is the most similar to Q depending on the size of Q for 300,000 token known samples and for four features, character 9-grams, frame 4-grams, POS 5-grams and word 2-grams. Each graph belongs to one of the top-performing measures (Cole, Consonni-Todeschini 5, Kulczynski, Phi, Simpson, Yule, and Cosine Delta for reference).

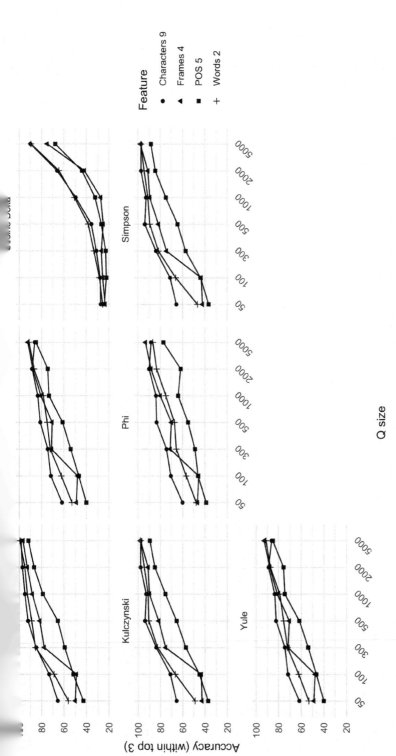

Figure 11 Percentage of times that the correct author is within the top three most similar authors to Q depending on the size of Q for 300,000 token known samples and for four features, character 9-grams, frame 4-grams, POS 5-grams and word 2-grams. Each graph belongs to one of the top-performing coefficients (Cole, Consonni-Todeschini 5, Kulczynski, Phi, Simpson, Yule, and Cosine Delta for reference).

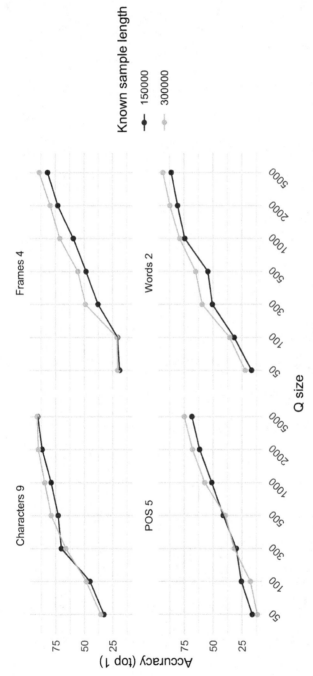

Figure 12 Accuracy of identification for Simpson coefficient for the four features (character 9-grams, word 2-grams, frames 4-grams, and POS 5-grams), different lengths of Q, and two known sample sizes, 150,000 tokens or 300,000 tokens.

incontrovertible evidence of a widely generalisable phenomenon and replications are therefore necessary.

For this reason, Experiment 2 is designed as a replication experiment involving modern data and it was carried out only *after* the results of the previous experiments were obtained. Thus, this study can be seen as a pre-registered study, with the previous results providing the hypotheses to confirm. The goal of this second experiment is to verify whether the same conclusions that were obtained in the *refcor* corpus are also found in a completely different and unrelated data set including modern data.

The corpus chosen for this experiment is the *c50* corpus (Houvardas and Stamatatos, 2006), which contains 50 authors, each having 100 documents, 50 for training and 50 for test, sampled from the corporate and industrial news category of the Reuters Corpus, Volume 1 (Lewis *et al.*, 2004). All texts in this corpus are therefore sampled from compatible registers because most of the aspects of the situation of production are compatible. The reason why this corpus was chosen is twofold: firstly, it contains many possible candidates and a substantial amount of data for each author, which is necessary to test the most extreme parameters of known sample size; secondly, the *c50* corpus has been used by several independent authorship analysis studies and it is therefore possible to compare the present results to those.

3.5.1 Previous Studies Using the c50 Corpus

The first authorship analysis study conducted on *c50* was Houvardas and Stamatatos (2006), who achieved about 75% accuracy overall using a support vector machine classifier on character n-grams. Then, Plakias and Stamatatos (2008) extracted the top ten most prolific authors in *c50* and, when considering ten authors, using a support vector machine trained with character 3-grams they achieve an overall accuracy of 80%. The next study found was López-Monroy *et al.* (2012), who also used this reduced version. They tested a technique based on automatic semantic classification of texts using either word or character n-gram frequencies, which achieved an overall accuracy of about 80%. Sapkota's *et al.* (2015) study on the complete *c50* obtained about 70% accuracy when training a support vector machine on character 3-grams.[7] A few recent studies applied even more sophisticated techniques. Sari *et al.* (2017) learned word embeddings with a neural network to reach a best accuracy of 72.6%.

---

[7] Sapkota *et al.* (2015) also removed quotations and signatures from the texts. In the version of the *c50* used for this study, no signatures of the authors were found after manual inspection. Quotations were not removed but, although this could affect the results, this operation was also not done in any other studies.

Similarly, Jafariakinabad and Hua (2021) used a self-supervised neural network learning algorithm annotated using syntactic structure to improve the performance to 83%. Murauer and Specht (2021) tested several methods, including the most sophisticated language models, and the highest F1 value they obtained was 70%. Finally, the latest study found at the time of writing is Dugar *et al.* (2022), who reached between 79% and 91% accuracy with language models such as FastText or GloVe. Their best performance of 91% was reached using FastText and a neural network with 768 hidden layers.

3.5.2 Methodology

The test carried out in this Experiment 2 is the same as for the *refcor* corpus. The only difference is that the known samples for this test were generated using the 50 texts of known authorship used for training in other studies. Thus, instead of taking an equal amount of data as a sample from each author, all their training data was used to make their known samples, which on average comprised 28,000 tokens. The mean and median length of these texts is roughly 560 but the minimum length is 58 and the maximum length is 1595. The remaining 50 texts per author originally used for test were used as *Q* texts. The mean/median length of these texts is 580, with similar minimum and maximum lengths as the known texts. The same feature types and the same coefficients tested in Experiment 1 were adopted, as one of the goals of this second experiment is to verify that the same results are obtained in modern data.

3.5.3 Results

The results in *c50* confirm the conclusions reached using *refcor*, as demonstrated by the heatmap in Figure 13, a replication of Figure 7.

This figure shows the same coefficients and features being the best for both corpora, with just slight variations. Some binary coefficients are again better than Cosine or Evert's Delta. For *c50*, it seems that it is harder to detect which coefficient is the best since many of them perform equally well and are able to detect the correct author within the top ten most similar author to the *Q* text. Regarding features, again short word n-grams and long character n-grams are the best ones, followed by frames and then POS. It is hard to understand which features are the best specifically but the important point is that the overall pattern is confirmed. The results demonstrate that the tendencies discovered in *refcor* generalise to an unseen modern data set.

To compare these results to previous studies, Table 8 shows the top ten configurations of coefficients and features with the highest percentages of accuracy, plus the best results for frames and POS n-grams for comparison.

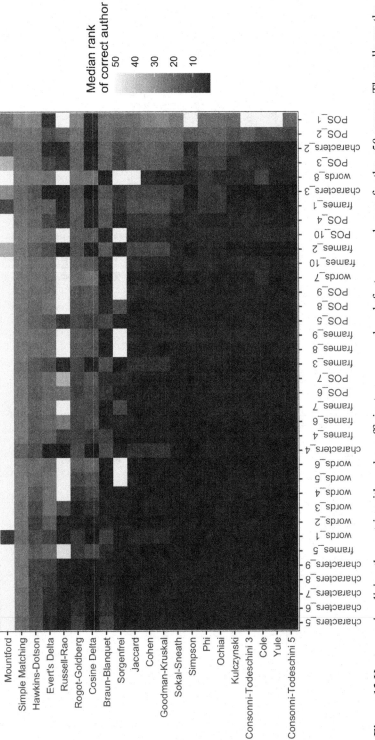

Figure 13 Heatmap visualising the matrix with each coefficient as rows and each feature as columns for the *c50* corpus. The cells are the median rank for each combination of coefficient and feature. Rows and columns are ordered by rank.

Table 8 Top ten performing feature and coefficient configurations in terms of percentage of times that the correct author is top or within the top three. In addition, the best-performing configuration with the frames and POS n-gram types are displayed for comparison.

Rank	Feature	Coefficient	% top 1	Rank	Feature	Coefficient	% top 3
1	words 3	Cole	73.2	1	words 3	Phi	91.36
2	words 3	Phi	72.96	2	words 3	Cole	91.32
3	words 3	Kulczynski	72.24	3	words 3	Kulczynski	90.8
4	characters 9	Phi	72	4	characters 9	Phi	90.72
5	characters 8	Phi	71.88	5	characters 8	Phi	90.64
6	words 3	Simpson	71.44	6	words 2	Phi	90.64
7	characters 7	Phi	70.92	7	words 3	Simpson	90.32
8	words 2	Phi	70.72	8	characters 9	Cole	89.84
9	words 2	Cole	70.28	9	characters 7	Phi	89.76
10	characters 9	Cole	70.2	10	words 2	Cole	89.6
...			...	...			...
46	frames 4	Cole	59.2	50	frames 4	Cole	79.24
...			...	...			...
90	POS 5	Phi	48	88	POS 5	Phi	68.16

These results are very surprising because the accuracy levels of this experiment are more or less the same as the ones obtained using machine learning and are comparable if not equal to the performance of very complex and computationally demanding neural network approaches.

A small difference between the two studies is that, compared to *refcor*, for *c50* it seems that even rather long word/punctuation n-grams are useful. This could be because there is a lot of formulaic language in the corpus. A manual inspection largely confirms this hypothesis as there are several word/punctuation 7-grams shared by authors between their training sample and the test sample, even though there are no duplicate texts in the corpus. Table 9 shows a random selection of these 7-grams.

Although it could be argued that topic is having an impact here, this is actually not correct. The longer an n-gram is, the less likely is its re-occurrence due to topic. These are therefore original encodings of meaning that the author repeats in similar circumstances. For example, there are six different authors that use the word *July* with *colony* within 5 words to the left or the right or there are three authors that use the word *controls* or *control* with *software* within 5 words to left or right. None of these authors, however, uses the exact same 7-gram. The objection to this argument is that certain words contained in the 7-grams are topical and are indeed found only in texts written by a certain author, for example *SATO* or *Internet Society*. These problems of the *c50* corpus are not easy to address because they are intrinsic to the data set. However, the present experiment can be directly compared to all other studies that worked on this same corpus and that could therefore exploit the formulaic nature of this register.

The only results for which it is guaranteed that topic information is ignored are frame and POS n-grams. Although their position in the ranking in Table 8 is low, it is important to notice that these results are way better than chance and that they are not

Table 9 Random selection of word/ punctuation 7-grams only found in common between an author's training texts and the same author's test texts.

the internet society, which helps develop
sato, an analyst at ubs securities
at the start of this year.
, ' said mms international analyst katherine
estimates from first call. Reporting dates
july, when the british colony of
software that controls the basic functions of

Table 10 List of random examples of frame 4-grams and POS 5-grams that are found in at least two texts, one training and one test, belonging to only one author.

Frame 4-grams	POS 5-grams
[NN NNS VBP *excessive*]	[, VBP JJ CD NNS]
[*domestic* NNS *who* VBP]	[VB NNP NNS TO IN]
[*due mainly to lower*]	[DT NN VBD A CD]
[NNS *that previously* VBD]	[POS CD NNS VBD NN]
[VBZ VBN *the chinese*]	[, WP NNS VBP VBG]
[NNS VBD *by three*]	[NN IN NNP RB NN]
[*that what* VBZ *up*]	[DT NNP VBD CD NNP]
[*in an antitrust* NN]	[DT NNP TO DT NN]
[VBD *almost one* NN]	[WDT VBZ NNP NNP TO]
[NN *during* NNP *and*]	[IN JJR NN CC JJ]

too far off from the state-of-the-art performance of machine learning techniques. When using frame 4-grams with Cole the correct author is first about 60% of the time (and within the top three 79% of the time), while using POS 5-grams with Phi the correct author is top almost half of the time (and within the top three 70% of the time). Table 10 presents a selection of random n-grams of these two types that are found across training and test texts for only one author. These n-grams, which largely have nothing to do with topic, can be considered either real grammatical units belonging to the grammar of the author or very close proxies to these units.

In conclusion, it is fair to say that the results observed for the *refcor* corpus are not just idiosyncratic to the Gutenberg novels because the findings generalise to an unseen modern data set. The fact that these *c50* texts are more formulaic means that the details of the results are slightly different but the general patterns hold. Most importantly, these results suggest that there is no substantial loss in performance using a method based on this theory compared to machine learning or neural network approaches that use frequency information. This finding is worthy of further scrutiny and can be considered evidence in favour of the Statistical Approximation Hypothesis.

3.6 Experiment 3: The Likelihood Ratio Framework

To bring this theory to fruition for real-life forensic linguistic casework, the likelihood ratio approach, which is the standard way in which forensic sciences present their results, should be adopted.

The role of the forensic scientist in court is to help the trier of fact's determination and the likelihood ratio represents the forensic scientist's contribution which the trier of fact, typically the jury, uses to arrive at their determination. During a trial, jurors hear a number of witnesses and at the end they express their judgement on whether the defendant is or is not guilty. We can call this final expression of judgement using Bayesian statistics terminology the *posterior odds*. The way the jury reaches this conclusion is by adjusting these odds as they hear more about the case and the evidence. Each bit of evidence moves the final posterior odds in favour of the prosecution or defence hypothesis according to its strength. This probability adjustment is the contribution of each piece of evidence and, mathematically speaking, is measured by the likelihood ratio. The forensic expert is not concerned about the initial (or *prior*) odds or the posterior odds: their job is just to present the evidence relevant to their expertise so that they can help the jury to adapt the odds of a guilty verdict accordingly.

Although this approach is well developed and used extensively in other forensic sciences, forensic authorship analysis is lagging behind. However, recent important work on the adoption of the likelihood ratio framework in the context of authorship analysis adopting a distance-based approach has been carried out by Ishihara (2021a) using Cosine Delta. As Carne and Ishihara (2021) argue, a *feature-based* method is theoretically and empirically superior to a *distance-based* method. The former implies the calculation of a likelihood ratio for each feature (e.g. word or n-gram) and then their fusion in a final likelihood ratio. The latter, instead, is based on one coefficient that summarises this variation. Despite the theoretical superiority, they conclude that the use of distance measures can often be more practical and easier to compute, a claim empirically confirmed by Ishihara (2021b).

To calculate likelihood ratios starting from a distance coefficient such as Cosine Delta or the binary coefficients examined in the present work, the following steps should be followed:

(1) A comparison data set of similar *background data* to the *test data* is compiled.
(2) The coefficient is calculated for all possible combinations of *same author* and *different author* in the background data.
(3) The two distributions of the coefficient for both same-author and different-author comparisons are extracted from the background data.
(4) The coefficient is calculated for all possible combinations of same author and different author in the test data.
(5) For each pair of either same-author or different-author in the test data, the likelihood ratio is calculated as the odds of obtaining that value in the case of same author vs different author for the background data.

(6) The resulting likelihood ratio expresses the odds of observing a certain value of the coefficient in the hypothesis that this coefficient is the result of a same-author comparison vs the hypothesis that this coefficient is the result of a different-author comparison.

This series of steps can be applied to any distance/similarity coefficient and the next section demonstrates this.

3.6.1 Calibration of Likelihood Ratios from Binary Coefficients

The calculation of a likelihood ratio needs (1) a background population from which to extract the distributions of coefficient values for same-author and different-author pairings; and (2) a different independent data set to test how useful the likelihood ratios are in predicting the origin of a comparison.

The present section reports on the results of two studies on the transformation of binary coefficients into likelihood ratios, a process called *calibration* (Ishihara, 2021a). In contrast to the other studies above, only some configurations of the testing parameters are selected: only the Simpson coefficient is used, as its fairly neutral assumptions make it an ideal starting point, and only some of the best performing features are considered: word 2-grams, character 9-grams, frames 4-grams, and POS 5-grams.

The first experiment is aimed at measuring if and how it is possible to take the 'known' half of the *c50* corpus as background data to then calculate the likelihood ratios for the 'unknown' half of the *c50*. Then, the second experiment verifies whether likelihood ratios for the 'unknown' *c50* can be useful if the background population is the *refcor* corpus, a corpus that is very different in terms of most situational characteristics. If it is possible to produce effective likelihood ratios that can be applied to modern data even when using mostly nineteenth-century novels, then one can speculate that these values of the Simpson coefficient are universal or, at the very least, that register variation can be substantially tolerated.

3.6.2 Experiment 3.1: c50 Background Data

In this first experiment, the training half of the *c50* is used to extract the distributions of the Simpson coefficient in the case in which the coefficient measures a different-author pair vs the case in which the coefficient measures a same-author pair. These distributions can be seen in Figure 14.

The density graphs clearly show how same-author comparisons result in higher values of the Simpson coefficient in all four feature types. Although the peaks for same-author comparisons vary slightly, from eyeballing the graph it would be fair

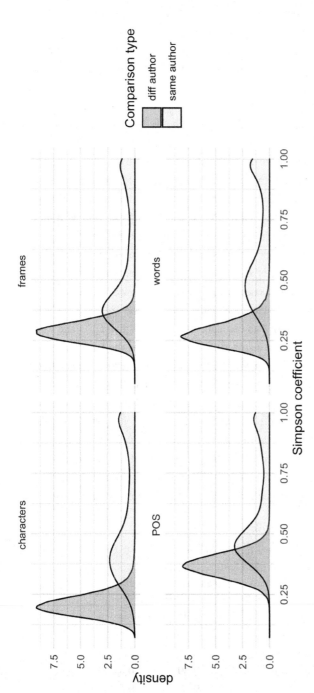

Figure 14 Density graphs showing the distribution of the Simpson coefficient for the four features considered (word 2-grams, character 9-grams, frame 4-grams, and POS 5-grams) for same-author comparisons *vs* different-author comparisons in the 'known' half of the *c50* corpus.

to conclude that if a comparison results in a Simpson coefficient larger than 0.5 it is very likely that this is because the candidate author is the author of the Q text. These odds can be expressed through a likelihood ratio.

This operation of calibration can be performed in various ways but, following Ishihara (2021a), the logistic regression method was applied here, as implemented by van Leeuwen (2015). In addition, rather than producing likelihood ratios, we adopt *log*-likelihood ratios, which have the advantage of expressing the ratio with a positive number if the evidence supports the same-author hypothesis or a negative number if the evidence supports the different-author hypothesis.

To assess the usefulness of these log-likelihood ratios we need the second half of the *c50* corpus. The background data is needed to generate a logistic regression model that transforms Simpson coefficients into log-likelihood ratios. The performance of this model is measured on the unseen half of the *c50* based on the extent to which these log-likelihood ratios make correct predictions.

The performance of a likelihood ratio is assessed by using a coefficient called C_{llr}. If the value of this coefficient is above 1, then this means that the information returned by the likelihood ratios is not useful. Any value below 1 instead means that there is useful information in the likelihood ratios and the closer the value of C_{llr} is to 0, the better. C_{llr} is made up of two components: $C_{llr} = C_{llr}^{min} + C_{llr}^{cal}$. The former measures the performance in terms of *discrimination* while the latter in terms of *calibration*. Table 11 shows the values of these performance metrics for this first test.

All the C_{llr} are indeed lower than 1, meaning that they provide useful information. The most effective features are word 2-grams and character 9-grams, as expected, even though we see that frames and POS do indeed contain useful information. The results can also be visualised in the form of Tippet plots, another standard way to report results about likelihood ratios.

Figure 15 shows the Tippet plot for word 2-grams only as an example. In this plot, the value of the log-likelihood ratio is on the horizontal axis and the

Table 11 Table indicating the values of C_{llr} and C_{llr}^{min} for each feature, all tested on *c50* with the first half of *c50* as background data.

	C_{llr}	C_{llr}^{min}
word 2-grams	0.30	0.29
character 9-grams	0.28	0.27
frame 4-grams	0.49	0.48
POS 5-grams	0.56	0.55

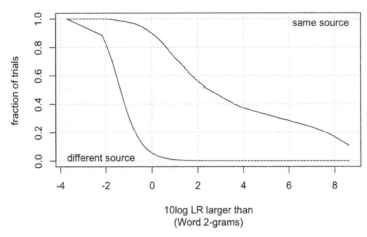

Figure 15 Tippet plots demonstrating the performance of the log-likelihood ratio for word 2-grams using the first half of *c50* as background data.

proportion of cases that score as much or greater on the vertical axis, with the two lines representing, on the right, same-author comparisons and, on the left, different-author comparisons. For example, we observe that almost 90% of same-author comparisons have a log-likelihood ratio above 0, which is only the case in less than 10% of different-author comparisons. Log-likelihood ratios equal to or greater than 2 are only obtained by same-author comparisons and never by different-author comparisons. The same distribution, in reverse, is seen for values lower than -2. We can therefore conclude that these results are well calibrated for this data set.

3.6.3 Experiment 3.2: refcor *Background Data*

The intent of the second experiment is instead to verify the generalisability of the findings of the first. The same procedure as above is repeated, with the exception that the background data is not the first half of *c50* but the *refcor* corpus. In order to make this computational experiment fair, only one configuration of Q and known sample length was selected: 500 tokens for Q length and 20,000 tokens for the known samples. In this way, the sizes are roughly the same across the two data sets. Apart from the similarity of size, however, the two data sets are rather different from each other, since *refcor* is mostly constituted by nineteenth-century novels.

Firstly, let's examine the distributions of the Simpson coefficient for each feature type in the *refcor*.

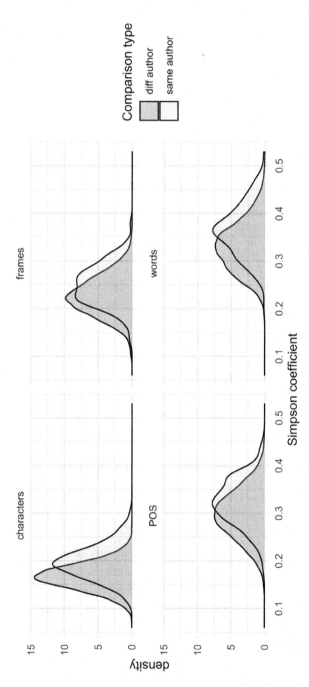

Figure 16 Density graphs showing the distribution of the Simpson coefficient for the four features considered (word 2-grams, character 9-grams, frame 4-grams, and POS 5-grams) for same-author comparisons vs different-author comparisons in the *refcor* corpus.

Table 12 Table indicating the values of C_{llr} and C_{llr}^{min} for each feature, all tested on *c50* with the *refcor* corpus used as background data.

	C_{llr}	C_{llr}^{min}
word 2-grams	0.43	0.29
character 9-grams	1.04	0.27
frame 4-grams	0.92	0.48
POS 5-grams	0.90	0.55

Figure 16 shows how the distributions in *refcor* are less skewed and look as if they are almost normally distributed, in contrast to *c50*. Although the difference is less prominent, in *refcor* we see again how same-author comparisons obtain scores for Simpson that are higher than different-author comparisons. Even though the shapes of the two distributions are different, it is possible to say that if a Simpson coefficient is greater than 0.4 then it is more likely that the comparison is a same-author comparison. In other words, a similarity of that magnitude is only likely if the Q text has been written by the same author from whom we extracted the known sample. The test to determine if this is a correct guess is again the evaluation of how useful the likelihood ratios are in measuring these odds.

The performance results are presented in Table 12. Except for character 9-grams, all other features have values of C_{llr} lower than 1. These scores are larger than in Experiment 1, meaning that the performance is poorer, which is not surprising. The only exception is word 2-grams, where actually the $C_{llr} = 0.43$ is not at all incompatible with the values found in Experiment 1.

The fact that there is a detectable signal even when the background data is so different is a surprising finding. The inconsistency between C_{llr} and C_{llr}^{min} suggests that this poor performance is due to lack of calibration, not lack of discrimination. As before, the Tippet plot in Figure 17 shows what these performance metrics mean in the case of word 2-grams. This Tippet plot is quite similar to the one in Figure 15 obtained when *c50* is used as background data

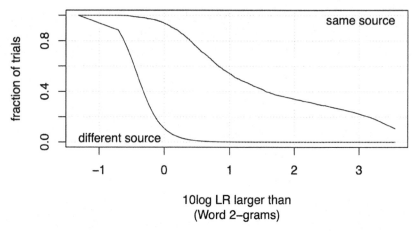

Figure 17 Tippet plots demonstrating the performance of the log-likelihood ratios for word 2-grams using *refcor* as background data.

3.6.4 Conclusions

The results demonstrate how the present cognitive linguistic Theory of Linguistic Individuality leads to applications that can then be adapted to the likelihood ratio framework. This is clearly shown for the *c50* corpus, where the likelihood ratios extracted from the first half perform very well in the unseen second half. However, the fact that it is possible to produce useful likelihood ratios for modern data starting from Project Gutenberg novels written a century ago is suggestive of the possibility that these probability distributions of the binary coefficients are somehow stable or that they can at least tolerate a lot of background noise. These results could indicate that a certain amount of similarity between a *Q* text and a known sample can only be found if they both come from the same author, almost as if there are thresholds after which the similarity between two samples is so great that we must conclude that they were produced by the same individual. This is an intriguing possibility that will have to be confirmed in future research.

4 Discussion

The last section presented a series of computational experiments that demonstrated how the theory introduced in Section 2 can be implemented for authorship analysis and for the provision of forensic evidence. These studies are not conclusive on their own. More experiments and replications are needed, especially without the various simplifications of the theory here adopted. This section contains a reflection on the implications of the results for the Theory.

4.1 The Cognitive Reality of n-grams and the Individuality Equilibrium

In much of recent computational research in authorship analysis, word n-grams, POS n-grams, and long character n-grams have largely been ignored. When their frequency is used, word or part-of-speech n-grams simply do not work as well as single words or short character n-grams. Antonia *et al.* (2014), who considered the frequency of n-grams precisely because of their cognitive realism, also concluded that single words are indeed more effective than n-grams.

Although cognitive realism is not much discussed in modern authorship analysis, the current state of the art seems to suggest a false opposition between scientific plausibility and efficiency. However, if instead of counting how many times a feature occurs the presence or absence of a feature is considered, then n-grams either outperform or perform as well as traditional frequency-based methods. This is a significant finding because it opens the way to authorship analysis methods that are both cognitively plausible, justified theoretically, explainable, and, with more research, also effective and efficient.

In this study, the features that were selected to approximate a linguistic unit are simple n-grams. As explained in the theory, a set is only a rough approximation to a real mental grammar, since the way a mental grammar is modelled in cognitive linguistics is as a network. However, the representation used in this work is more plausible than the traditional model used in authorship analysis of a bag-of-words. Thus, in addition to the theoretical arguments in its favour, the successful results of the studies above point to this set of n-grams model being, at the very least, a good enough approximation to reality despite this simplification. This is especially the case for long character n-grams. Following cognitive linguistics, this theory predicts that the word does not have special unit status in a person's grammar. The fact that character 9-grams are the best feature generally speaking can be seen as a confirmation of how a usage-based cognitive linguistic theory of language is a valid one for authorship analysis. The use of characters allows the identification of units that are both plausible and distinctive enough for each author but that would not be captured if a traditional grammatical segmentation or tokenisation is adopted.

The computational experiments above also suggest how the fewer atomic elements to form an n-gram there are, the larger is the n you need to achieve good accuracy. These results are in line with what is predicted by the constraints on human working memory predicted by well-established cognitive psychology theories. The fact that the size of each of the best n-gram features is compatible with the predictions made by these cognitive theories is encouraging because it is suggestive that these units could be real mental units. The fact that these units can distinguish authors is consequently explainable by the Principle of Linguistic Individuality.

N-grams range from short sequences that are very common (character 2-grams) to very long n-grams that tend to be unique even for the individual who uses them (word 7-grams). For an authorship analysis method based on binary coefficients, the performance is poor for both of these types of n-gram but the range between these two points will be like a parabola, with a peak signalling the best n-gram length to capture individuality. These n-grams are in the 'Goldilocks zone' of the linguistic individuality space: they do not appear in everyone's grammar so as to be useless, yet they are not so rare and unique as to only be uttered once and never repeated. Instead, they recur just enough in the language of an author to make it identifiable. This sweet spot of individuality is like an equilibrium between absolute pervasiveness and absolute uniqueness, and it varies in a predictable fashion depending on the feature type.

The hypothesis put forward to explain this effect is that when an n-gram is short and common, then it is likely that the n-gram is not a real linguistic unit for an individual but a *sub-component* of a unit. For example, character 1-grams are unlikely to be units but they are definitely components of units. Similarly, a word 10-gram is unlikely to be a unit and more likely to be a structure containing linguistic units, thus a unique creation that an individual would not and could not store because of working memory constraints. Instead, n-grams such as word 2-grams or character 9-grams or POS 5-grams are the right size to be realistic units because they are convenient enough to be memorised for reuse.

Another tentative conclusion is that the peak of this individuality equilibrium changes with the register. We can propose this conclusion because, for example, the best n for n-grams in *c50* is slightly larger than for *refcor*. A potential explanation could be that the more idiomatic and repetitive a register is, the more likely it is that individuals process it in larger chunks, as this way of processing would be more advantageous in those cases.

All in all, despite their simplicity, it is possible that n-grams are relatively good approximations to real linguistic units. However, new methods based on this theory should also consider more flexible and comprehensive sequences as candidate units instead. The grammar induction function used is in itself a way to test various hypotheses of how the linguistic individual processes language. The function used in this work is quite basic and does not allow for units of various sizes to be extracted. However, better functions would select units of variable sizes, as long as certain requirements, potentially cognitively realistic ones, are met.

4.2 Evidence for the Statistical Approximation Hypothesis

This notion of an individuality equilibrium is very well connected to the Statistical Approximation Hypothesis introduced in Section 2.4. In a nutshell, this hypothesis proposes that frequency-based methods for authorship analysis are essentially a numeric summary of a G_t. If this is true, then what explains our ability to identify an author, even when using frequency methods, is still the Principle of Linguistic Individuality. The only difference is that, when using Delta, instead of measuring G_t directly a statistical imprint of this unique grammar is captured through word or character counts. The prediction made by this hypothesis is therefore that a more direct method of capturing the grammar of an individual should be equally good or superior in performance to the frequency methods.

This is precisely what is seen in the studies reported above. Especially in the results for the *c50* corpus, methods introduced in this work based on binary coefficients of n-grams perform equally well if not better than methods using frequency and far more complex statistical procedures, such as machine learning algorithms. In addition, another important pattern uncovered in these studies is the complementarity of the binary coefficients and Delta. For example, when the character n-grams are short then Delta works well and binary coefficients do not. When, instead, the character n-grams are long it is the binary coefficients that work well while Delta fails. The performance of Delta decreases gradually as the performance of the binary coefficients increases. In other words, Delta works very well only when a sub-section of the space of features is considered, typically the one composed of the top most frequent words, which tend to be, precisely, *sub-units* that constitute larger n-grams, which are instead more likely to be real mental units. This fascinating phenomenon is therefore remarkably suggestive of what should be observed if the hypothesis was correct: the frequency of sub-units stops being useful when considering presence/absence of full units because the information being picked up is the same.

This is only a tentative conclusion, however, since this pattern could also have other explanations. For example, it is possible that frequency methods using character 2-grams and Phi using character 9-grams are complementary because they capture useful but different information about authorship which is not captured by the other. Or it is possible that the Principle of Linguistic Individuality is responsible for only some of the variation in functor frequencies, while other aspects of linguistic individuality, which are not covered by the present theory, contribute to explaining the rest of the variation. The only way to answer these questions is through more empirical work.

4.3 Capturing an Individual Grammar in Full

The (un)feasibility of collecting an entire individual's grammar was addressed theoretically in Section 2.3.1 in relation to Herdan–Heaps' law. After the empirical studies above, it is possible to advance this discussion a little further by reflecting on a few key points. Firstly, the empirical explorations revealed that, in contrast to traditional frequency-based methods for which the addition of more features does not lead to improvement in performance, for the authorship analysis methods based on binary coefficients the more features the better. Secondly, although an improvement was noted when reaching 300,000 tokens, at least for the *refcor* corpus we have evidence that 150,000 tokens are almost as good as 300,000.

The latter result precisely reflects the consequences of the Herdan–Heaps' law for authorship analysis. After 150,000 tokens, adding the same amount over again to the known sample leads to very little difference in identification performance, which seems to suggest that a critical level corresponding to the coverage of the core grammar has been hit. It would be difficult to imagine that reaching, for example, one million tokens for an author would massively change the results and we know this because of Herdan–Heaps' law. In sum, at least for *refcor*, we have a threshold after which we can say that we captured the closest approximation to the full grammar of an individual, at least for one particular register. Although these 150,000 tokens do not exactly contain the entirety of the grammar of a person for a register, they are a good enough approximation for authorship analysis because they might represent the core grammar of the individual.

Another important point emerging from these studies is that a large amount of comparison data can compensate for small disputed texts. The results show how even texts as short as 50 words could be attributed much better than chance as long as hundreds of thousands of words of data are available for comparison. This is a very important finding for authorship analysis and points to the far greater importance of having a large comparison data set than a large questioned data set.

In conclusion, there are two take-home messages for authorship analysis that should be considered for further scrutiny. The first is that, contrary to what has been hypothesised until now, it is actually possible to capture a very close approximation to a person's grammar. We do not know yet whether this approximation only concerns one single register or if these thresholds are register-specific but we know that it is possible, a fact that should encourage more studies on other types of data. The second message is that, once these known samples are created, then the length of the Q text is not as important.

4.4 The Evaluation of Similarity

The importance of being able to weight the linguistic similarities between two sets of texts has been extensively pointed out by scholars in forensic linguistics. For example, Solan and Tiersma (2005, pp. 163–4) noted that 'pointing out the similarities between documents without taking into account the likelihood of such overlap, especially by people in the academic community, and without any analysis of the differences between the authors, is not good science' and that 'without taking base rates into account, it is impossible to know how much to make of each observed similarity'. Similarly, Coulthard (2004, pp. 444–5) wrote: 'work by many people on a large number of cases has shown that there is no longer any dispute that the occurrence of shared identical items is conclusive evidence that two texts have not been independently created; what remains to be agreed is how few shared identical items are necessary to support a decision'.

Firstly, the present studies demonstrate that pointing out the similarities alone is actually not enough. The most successful binary coefficients, like Phi or Cole, included information about negative matches, or common absences. This was especially true for the cases including large comparison samples, suggesting that once a large amount of data is available, then absences of features are indeed evidence of absence in an individual's grammar. Thus, in contrast to a priori speculations, empirical evidence demonstrates that absences have a role to play in authorship analysis.

Secondly, the studies also demonstrate that the advancement called for by Solan and Tiersma (2005) and Coulthard (2004) must and can be done using the likelihood ratio framework. The likelihood ratio analysis demonstrated in Section 3.6 is precisely a way to evaluate the shared similarities between two samples, one being the Q text and the other the sample of a known author, compared against the baseline of what is similarity by chance in a comparable sample. The likelihood ratio is therefore the way to express numerically and then verbally how much to make of the observed similarity. Much more research must be done in this area to arrive at standards of practice that are widely agreed upon. However, the studies in Section 3.6 and their promising results should pave the way for conducting further work in the near future.

Although the assumption about the values associated with these thresholds of similarity should be that they vary case by case, at least for now the results of Section 3.6 show us that there could be more universality in it than one could in principle assume. The fact that thresholds obtained from nineteenth-century data work for modern texts in another register is at the very least surprising. And yet, to a certain extent, the results can be justified theoretically by the Principle of Linguistic Individuality: if individuality in language is pervasive and considerable and our feeling that we all use the same grammar is an illusion, then it makes sense that two independently produced texts have very low thresholds of similarity compared to two texts produced by the same author. Although this critical threshold will vary depending on the coefficient and the feature type used, its existence can be verified relatively quickly once more evidence is available through replication of this study over many different data sets. In the a priori unlikely case that 'universal' thresholds of similarity exist, then one could foresee a future where the forensic linguist can immediately evaluate whether doing a full analysis is advisable or not by simply measuring the similarity, even without calculating a likelihood ratio.

In conclusion, though, whatever future empirical studies will show, it is undeniable that the move from authorship analysis to *forensic* authorship analysis can only happen with the adoption of the likelihood ratio framework, especially as this is readily applicable as demonstrated in this work.

4.5 An Individual's Grammar As a Behavioural Biometric

A *biometric* is a measurement of a *physiological* or *behavioural* human feature that meets four properties (Jain et al., 2004):

(1) *universality*: each individual has the feature;
(2) *distinctiveness*: each individual is different in regard to this feature;
(3) *permanence*: the feature is invariant over time;
(4) *collectability*: the feature can be measured.

We can then define a *biometric system* as a set of methodologies and tools to use a biometric to identify individuals. Jain *et al.* (2004) list various physiological and behavioural biometrics, such as DNA, fingerprints, gait, iris and retina, vein patterns on a hand, voice, and signatures.

The argument that authorship analysis is a biometric system is not new. Narayanan *et al.* (2012, p. 4), for example, wrote that 'stylometric fingerprints can be considered a [*sic*] extension of behavioral biometrics'. Similarly, Pokhriyal *et al.* (2017) claimed that the extraction of stylometric markers constitutes a *cognitive biometric*, even though they do not refer to any research that has to do with writing, linguistics, or cognitive science.

Although this and other studies called for stylometry to be listed as biometric, this is technically and theoretically incorrect because stylometry is not the biometric itself, the feature being measured, but only a biometric system, the tools through which we measure a characteristic. The missing piece that seems to be ignored is: what human biometric characteristic is measured with stylometry? This is not a trivial question because it is not possible to conclude that whatever these 'stylometric fingerprints' measure is a biometric without an understanding of what is being measured.

The argument proposed in this section is that the present Theory of Linguistic Individuality allows us to rightly call authorship analysis a biometric system measuring a specific behavioural biometric of an individual, their G_t. If we understand linguistic individuality as an emerging property of an individual connected to the development of their unique repository of lexicogrammatical units, then we can also check how and to what extent the criteria for a biometric are met for G_t. The Principle of Linguistic Individuality tells us how G_t meets the first three criteria for a window of time t. Cognitive usage-based linguistics provides evidence that language is a learned behaviour and it also explains why and how individuals differ in the creation of their own personalised mental grammar. The last criterion of *collectability* has been demonstrated empirically in this work but it is generally speaking work in progress as new and better ways to approximate G_t are developed over time. It is therefore this link to the science of language that enables us to say with confidence that authorship analysis can be classified as a behavioural biometric system.

4.6 What About Style?

The elephant in the room of the present Element is the concept of *style*. As it stands, the present theory does not include this notion, which is, however, a concept called upon relatively often in research in authorship analysis. How does *style* fit into this theory?

As explained in Section 1, style is linked to register: a style is a variety, so a constellation of linguistic features, that is associated with a social group, community, or individual when producing a text in a particular communicative situation. This definition of style is compatible with the functional linguistics tradition, such as work done by Biber (1988) and Biber and Conrad (2009) but also Halliday and Matthiessen (2004) and Hasan (2009b, 2009a). This tradition teaches us how style and register are not in an additive relationship: one cannot simply subtract register from a text and get the style. Instead, a style can be seen as a register that belongs to a group. For example, let's take academic prose. If one collects a large sample of academic texts, all the constellation of linguistic features that they have in common could be called the register of academic texts. However, if one collects academic texts written by undergraduate students, one is observing the way this group interacts with the context, thus getting the register of a social group, which is what we call a style. Similarly, if one collects academic texts written by a group of individuals who have never encountered this type of text then the variety of language they produce is going to be their style of academic text. In reality, a better term for this type of *style* is *code*, as proposed by Hasan (1996) and applied to authorship analysis by Nini and Grant (2013).

That the notion of style is insufficient and unrealistic to characterise author- ship analysis can be confirmed by carrying out a thought experiment on what constitutes a 'stylistic choice', as in McMenamin's (2002) sense. Let us assume that an individual selects the word *get* as opposed to *obtain* because they have never come across the latter; can we call this a stylistic *choice*? Or, alternatively, can an individual who uses the double-object construction *give me it*, which is attested in northern dialects of British English, be compared to other individuals who are native speakers of other varieties of English for whom this construction is deemed ungrammatical? Or again, in the example above of undergraduate students writing academic prose, to what extent can their overuse of complex sentences as opposed to complex noun phrases be called a stylistic *choice* rather than a lack of familiarity with these structures due to lack of exposure? If a choice is not in someone's repertoire, then it cannot possibly be called a 'choice' at all for that person.

Modelling individuality as the result of stylistic choices implies that we all have all options at our disposal and we select the ones we want to use. This conceptualisation of idiolect, which is consistent with Turell's notion of *idio- lectal style*, would model a person's idiolect as the personalised sets of choices among several options. However, as demonstrated by the above thought experi- ments, this understanding of individuality is not necessarily realistic in all situations. Instead, given what we know from cognitive usage-based linguistics studies about language production, it is actually more likely that very often we do not have so much of a choice of what to say because our language production is a reflection of the level of entrenchment of the units that make up our grammar.

For the reasons outlined above, continuing to think about authorship analysis as the comparison of styles is simply untenable linguistically and scientifically. The implications of this conclusion for authorship analysis is that, unlike Kestemont's (2014) analogy, authorship analysis should not be akin to Morelli's method of recognising painters from the way they painted ears, noses, leaves, clouds, or other elements that are frequent but not essential. How does style fit in in this theory, then? The answer is in all likelihood that some of the aspects that are typically called 'style' in the context of authorship analysis are instead better explained by the Principle of Linguistic Individuality and the theory outlined in this work. This is particularly the case for what McMenamin (2002) calls 'habits' that make up our style.

Having said that, though, because of the nature of language production in writing, the present theory might not fully account for all authorial information in a text. For example, it is very common for an author to write a piece of text and then go back and change it. Perhaps the author looks up a word in a dictionary and substitutes it with another word and so on. All these mechanics of revision are not taken into account in the present theory, which instead focuses exclusively on the act of producing language in the moment.

It is therefore possible that something akin to the naive understanding of style, such as the notion of aesthetically acceptable or unacceptable, could still play a part in authorship analysis and, if that is the case, this aspect should be included in any future expansion of this theory. The way this must be done, however, is again by including insight from cognitive science and established scientific knowledge of the act of writing a text. Although there is not much research on cognitive models of linguistic production in writing, the available models suggest that writing consists of two major phases: *translation* and *editing* (Galbraith, 2009). The former is the process of converting ideas into words and it is likely that the factors explored above in relation to cognitive linguistics explain this process of linguistic production. The editing phase, instead, is a more conscious process that works very differently. This distinction could hold in the future and lead to a differentiation between the selection of entrenched units on the one hand and the choice of style markers on the other. The notion of stylistic choice, which is not valid for the translation phase, could instead apply to style markers that emerge during the editing phase. All in all, more research to disentangle these two types of evidence is needed. For example, it is likely that at least for forensic purposes it is better to focus on translation-generated markers than editing-generated marks, as the latter could be in principle easier to disguise or imitate. This unresolved matter leaves plenty of room for further expansions and enhancements of the present work.

4.7 A New Perspective on Authorship Analysis

The final reflection is on the consequences of this theory and the evidence above for the way authorship analysis is conceived. As previously explained, the present theory suggests that we can abandon the notion of authorship analysis as 'style detection'. In addition, cognitive linguistics and cognitive science reveal how Mosteller and Wallace's (1963) implicit model of language production as a word-by-word choice is untenable. Interestingly, as demonstrated empirically in this work, a method of authorship analysis grounded on cognitive theories of language processing instead looks much more similar to the methods commonly employed to tackle plagiarism.

The point being made here is that authorship analysis should be reinterpreted from 'style analysis' to a kind of plagiarism detection. This follows logically from this theory. If each individual has a unique repertoire of units, then recognising an author is like detecting self-plagiarism. The empirical component of this work indeed implemented a very simple comparison of common n-grams, which is the classic and most straightforward way to test for plagiarism. The only difference was the size of the n-grams. For evidence of plagiarism, common n-grams longer than the ones that work for authorship analysis are needed. This is because, as empirically shown, once a sequence reaches a certain length then this becomes unique to the author as well, making it therefore a unique fingerprint of the text produced by this person. The mechanics of authorship analysis is not far from that, though, as the present work demonstrated how collections of shorter sequences equally become 'linguistic fingerprints' of an author.

For this reason, another important prediction of the present theory is that better success in authorship analysis will be achieved with techniques that are similar to the ones currently employed in plagiarism detection. In this field, brute force common n-grams detection has been superseded by more complex but efficient techniques, such as fingerprinting or alignments algorithms also used in genetics (Oakes, 2014). Although these techniques as they stand cannot function for authorship analysis, if this theory holds true it should be possible to tweak them to more efficiently and accurately capture the same kind of authorial signal detected in the present empirical studies. Ideally, the best techniques would be the ones that extend this approach to measure the actual entity being studied – that is, the author's grammar – such as techniques that extract networks of nested units rather than sequences.

5 Moving Forward

The present work began with an overview of the current state of the art of authorship analysis and the success of Delta, an outstanding fact about natural language that is still in search of plausible explanations. In order to arrive at such an explanation in a way that is compatible with modern understanding of language processing, in the present work it was suggested that we need to look at language in the way that is done in cognitive usage-based linguistics.

By explaining the fundamentals of this paradigm of research, the foundations for understanding the key notion of individuality in language were laid out in preparation for the introduction of a Theory of Linguistic Individuality. The cornerstones of this theory are that language can be seen as the union of individual mental grammars, which in turn are systematic and idiosyncratic repositories of units. This notion was then formalised in this theory as the Principle of Linguistic Individuality, which is claimed to be the foundational notion for a scientific and cognitively plausible authorship analysis practice. It is therefore claimed in this work that Delta works because it is a statistical approximation to a person's unique grammar, a hypothesis called the *Statistical Approximation Hypothesis*.

The rest of the work then demonstrated how the theory can be applied to authorship analysis, revealing evidence in favour of the statistical structure hypothesis but also, more generally, in favour of the theory's main tenets. Before drawing the necessary conclusions, a demonstration of how to convert the empirical application of the theory to the likelihood ratio framework was presented, thus creating a strong connection between theory and forensic practice.

This final concluding section is dedicated to outlining a plan for future research inspired by this paradigm.

5.1 A Research Agenda for Future Work

There are several lines of enquiry that the present theory leaves open for future studies. It is important to note that these questions existed even before the introduction of the present theory. However, the benefit of having this Theory of Linguistic Individuality is that these questions can now be contextualised and given a proper name. In this way, new knowledge is generated and scaffolded systematically so that progress is made in a precise direction.

What follows is therefore a list of research questions for the future. The answers to these questions would serve to confirm the theory and, if or where this fails, to expand it and modify it. The answers to these questions are of great benefit for both our understanding of linguistic individuality and for the practice in (forensic) authorship analysis.

(1) What is the value of t? This is one of the most important questions because the entire notion of the unique linguistic individual rests on this number. The value of t is essentially the length of the time window during which the

grammar of an individual G_t remains constant. Although we do not have data to even make a guess, we know that, at least in most cases, this window is quite large as otherwise we would not be able to make great progress in authorship analysis at all. This question is not going to be easy to answer but there is no doubt that, with laboratory experiments and longitudinal corpus analyses, some approximations can be obtained.

(2) How big is a G_t? Although we do know that the set of units that an individual can use is extremely large, we also know that it is not infinite. If it is not infinite, then there must be a number or at the very least an approximate magnitude of its size that we can estimate. Research of this kind for the lexicon is being carried out and we do have rough estimations of the size of individuals' lexicons. At the moment there is no research on the size of an individual's repository of units but there is no reason why this cannot be done in principle. Research on this aspect is marginally important for cognitive linguistics but it would be quite important for forensic linguistics and authorship analysis.

(3) How does Herdan–Heaps' law apply to G_t? Or, better, what is the relationship between unit types and unit tokens? This research would be important for authorship analysis because, as explained in Section 2.3.1, it would tell us at what point one can say confidently that collecting more data for an individual becomes unnecessary.

(4) Is there a critical entrenchment threshold after which an individual is more likely to use a particular unit? Langacker (1987) argued that this threshold does not exist and that entrenchment is a continuum. Although this is likely to be the case, it is still possible that there is a critical threshold that leads to a sudden higher probability of usage by an individual. If this exists, what is it? This is a very difficult question to answer but answering it would lead us closer to finding methods to extract realistic units. In the present work, the role of entrenchment has been put aside for the sake of simplification, an unrealistic but necessary assumption to carry out initial empirical work. However, the prediction made by this theory is that taking entrenchment into account should improve authorship analysis.

(5) Another simplification that was adopted for the present work is the treatment of grammars as sets as opposed to graphs. The obvious next step would therefore be the use of graph theory instead of set theory. This representation of grammar would be more realistic than the one portrayed here but also far more complex. Nonetheless, if the theory is right, authorship analysis methods based on graph theory should outperform the ones based on set theory.

(6) As anticipated in Section 4.6, a better integration of this theory with cognitive models of written language production should be pursued. Although the notion of style is not explored in this work, it is possible that it could feature in an expansion of this theory that is better integrated with known cognitive science facts about the process of writing.

(7) And, finally, a last but not least important question: is all this valid in other languages? The present work is only based on English and, although the theories and principles that are derived from cognitive linguistics should apply to any language, again this should be confirmed empirically.

5.2 Final Conclusions

In this Element, a Theory of Linguistic Individuality has been delineated with the goal of directing and encouraging future research in authorship analysis towards a direction that is both computationally successful and scientifically plausible. There is one consideration about the practice of authorship analysis that emerges from this work and that should be adopted in the future, especially but not exclusively in *forensic* authorship analysis: the foundation of the practice of authorship analysis should be based on the science of estimating the similarity between two samples of language. As such, it should rely on our knowledge of how much similarity is to be expected between two samples generated by the same grammar vs two samples generated by two different grammars given the conditions of production of the samples. However, for the field to move towards this goal, it is evident that we need to know more about the way texts are produced. Progress in this direction must advance fuelled by existing widely accepted understanding of human cognition.

5.3 Supplementary Material: Data and Code

The data and the R code used for the experiments can be found here: www.cambridge.org/nini.

References

Anthonissen, L. and Petré, P. (2019) 'Grammaticalization and the linguistic individual: New avenues in lifespan research', *Linguistics Vanguard*, 5(s2), pp. 20180037. Available at: https://doi.org/10.1515/lingvan-2018-0037.

Antonia, A., Craig, H., and Elliott, J. (2014) 'Language chunking, data sparseness, and the value of a long marker list: Explorations with word n-grams and authorial attribution', *Literary and Linguistic Computing*, 29(2), pp. 147–63. Available at: https://doi.org/10.1093/llc/fqt028.

Argamon, S. (2008) 'Interpreting Burrows's Delta: Geometric and probabilistic foundations', *Literary and Linguistic Computing*, 23(2), pp. 131–47. Available at: https://doi.org/10.1093/llc/fqn003.

Argamon, S. E. (2018) 'Computational forensic authorship analysis: Promises and pitfalls', *Language and Law / Linguagem e Direito*, 5(2), pp. 7–37.

Barlow, M. (2013) 'Individual differences and usage-based grammar', *International Journal of Corpus Linguistics*, 18(4), pp. 443–78. Available at: https://doi.org/10.1075/ijcl.18.4.01bar.

Beckner, C., Ellis, N. C., Blythe, R., *et al.* (2009) 'Language is a complex adaptive system: Position paper', *Language Learning*, 59, pp. 1–26.

Biber, D. (1988) *Variation across Speech and Writing*. Cambridge: Cambridge University Press.

Biber, D. (2009) 'A corpus-driven approach to formulaic language in English: Multi-word patterns in speech and writing', *International Journal of Corpus Linguistics*, 14(3), pp. 275–311.

Biber, D. and Conrad, S. (2009) *Register, Genre, and Style*. Cambridge: Cambridge University Press.

Bloch, B. (1948) 'A set of postulates for phonemic analysis', *Language*, 24(1), pp. 3–46.

Braun-Blanquet, J. (1932) *Plant Sociology: The Study of Plant Communities*. New York: McGraw-Hill.

Burrows, J. (2002) '"Delta": A measure of stylistic difference and a guide to likely authorship', *Literary and Linguistic Computing*, 17(3), p. 267.

Bybee, J. L. (2006) 'From usage to grammar: The mind's response to repetition', *Language*, 82(4), pp. 711–33. Available at: https://doi.org/10.1353/lan.2006.0186.

Bybee, J. (2010) *Language, Usage and Cognition*. Cambridge: Cambridge University Press.

Carne, M. and Ishihara, S. (2021) 'Feature-based forensic text comparison using a Poisson model for likelihood ratio estimation', in *Proceedings of the 18th Workshop of the Australasian Language Technology Association.* Australasian Language Technology Association, pp. 32–42.

Chaski, C. E. (2001) 'Empirical evaluations of language-based author identification techniques', *Forensic Linguistics*, 8(1), pp. 1–65.

Christiansen, M. H. and Chater, N. (2016) 'The Now-or-Never bottleneck: A fundamental constraint on language', *Behavioral and Brain Sciences*, 39, p. e62. Available at: https://doi.org/10.1017/S0140525X1500031X.

Cohen, J. (1960) 'A coefficient of agreement for nominal scales', *Educational and Psychological Measurements*, 20, pp. 37–46.

Cole, L. C. (1949) 'The measurement of interspecific association', *Ecology*, 30, pp. 411–24.

Consonni, V. and Todeschini, R. (2012) 'New similarity coefficients for binary data', *MATCH Communications in Mathematical and in Computer Chemistry*, 68, pp. 581–92.

Coulthard, M. (2004) 'Author identification, idiolect, and linguistic uniqueness', *Applied Linguistics*, 25, pp. 431–47.

Coulthard, M. (2013) 'On admissible linguistic evidence', *Journal of Law and Policy*, 21, pp. 441–66.

Coulthard, M., Johnson, A., and Wright, D. (2017) *An Introduction to Forensic Linguistics*. Abingdon: Routledge.

Cowan, N. (2001) 'The magical number 4 in short-term memory: A reconsideration of mental storage capacity', *Behavioral and Brain Sciences*, 24(1), pp. 87–114. Available at: https://doi.org/10.1017/S0140525X01003922.

Croft, W. (2001) *Radical Construction Grammar: Syntactic Theory in Typological Perspective*. Oxford: Oxford University Press. Available at: https://doi.org/10.1093/acprof:oso/9780198299554.001.0001.

Dąbrowska, E. (2012) 'Different speakers, different grammars', *Linguistic Approaches to Bilingualism*, 2(3), pp. 219–53. Available at: https://doi.org/10.1075/lab.2.3.01dab.

Dąbrowska, E. (2015) 'Individual differences in grammatical knowledge', in E. Dąbrowska and D. Divjak (eds.) *Handbook of Cognitive Linguistics*. Berlin: De Gruyter, pp. 650–67.

Dąbrowska, E. (2018) 'Experience, aptitude and individual differences in native language ultimate attainment', *Cognition*, 178 (May), pp. 222–35. Available at: https://doi.org/10.1016/j.cognition.2018.05.018.

Dąbrowska, E. (2020) 'Language as a phenomenon of the third kind', *Cognitive Linguistics*, 31(2), pp. 213–29. Available at: https://doi.org/10.1515/cog-2019-0029.

Daelemans, W. (2013) 'Explanation in computational stylometry', *Computational Linguistics and Intelligent Text Processing*, 7817(2), pp. 451–62.

Dasgupta, I. and Gershman, S. J. (2021) 'Memory as a computational resource', *Trends in Cognitive Sciences*, 25(3), pp. 240–51. Available at: https://doi.org/ 10.1016/j.tics.2020.12.008.

Diessel, H. (2019) *The Grammar Network: How Linguistic Structure is Shaped by Language Use*. Cambridge: Cambridge University Press.

Divjak, D. (2019) *Frequency in Language: Memory, Attention and Learning*. Cambridge: Cambridge University Press.

Driver, H. E. and Kroeber, A. L. (1932) 'Quantitative expression of cultural relationship', *University of California Publications in American Archaeology and Ethnology*, 31, pp. 211–56.

Dugar, T. K., Gowtham, S., and Chakraborty, U. Kr. (2022) 'Comparing word embeddings on authorship identification', in S. Borah and R. Panigrahi (eds.) *Applied Soft Computing: Techniques and Applications*. Boca Raton, FL: CRC Press, pp. 177–94.

Dunn, J. (2017) 'Computational learning of construction grammars', *Language and Cognition*, 9(2), pp. 254–92. Available at: https://doi.org/10.1017/ langcog.2016.7.

Dunn, J. and Nini, A. (2021) 'Production vs perception: The role of individuality in usage-based grammar induction', in *Proceedings of the Workshop on Cognitive Modeling and Computational Linguistics* (online), Association for Computational Linguistics. Available at: https://aclanthology.org/2021.cmcl-1.19/, pp. 149–59.

Eder, M. (2015) 'Does size matter? Authorship attribution, small samples, big problem', *Digital Scholarship in the Humanities*, 30(2), pp. 167–82. Available at: https://doi.org/10.1093/llc/fqt066.

Ellis, N. C. (2002) 'Frequency effects in language processing', *Studies in Second Language Acquisition*, 24(02), pp. 143–88. Available at: https://doi .org/10.1017/S0272263102002024.

Ellis, N. C., Römer, U., and O'Donnell, M. B. (2016) *Usage-Based Approaches to Language Acquisition and Processing: Cognitive and Corpus Investigations of Construction Grammar*. Malden, MA: Wiley-Blackwell.

Erman, B. and Warren, B. (2000) 'The idiom principle and the open choice principle', *Text*, 20(1), pp. 29–62. Available at: https://doi.org/10.1515/ text.1.2000.20.1.29.

Evert, S., Proisl, T., Vitt, T., *et al.* (2015) 'Towards a better understanding of Burrows's Delta in literary authorship attribution', in A. Feldman, A. Kazantseva, S. Szpakowicz, *et al.* (eds.) *Proceedings of the Fourth*

Workshop on Computational Linguistics for Literature. Denver, CO: Association for Computational Linguistics, pp. 79–88.

Evert, S., Proisl, T., Jannidis, F., *et al.* (2017) 'Understanding and explaining Delta measures for authorship attribution', *Digital Scholarship in the Humanities*, 32, pp. ii4–ii16. Available at: https://doi.org/10.1093/llc/fqx023.

Fedorenko, E. (2021) 'The human language system in the mind and brain', in *5th Usage-Based Linguistics Conference* (online), Tel Aviv University. Available at: https://youtu.be/edlY4GbH1tU .

Fonteyn, L. (2021) 'Constructional change across the lifespan of 20 early modern gentlemen', in *11th International Conference on Construction Grammar (ICCG11)*. Antwerp: University of Antwerp. Available at: https://doi.org/10.5281/zenodo.5220179.

Fonteyn, L. and Nini, A. (2020) 'Individuality in syntactic variation: An investigation of the seventeenth-century gerund alternation', *Cognitive Linguistics*, 31(2), pp. 279–308. Available at: https://doi.org/10.1515/COG-2019-0040.

Galbraith, D. (2009) 'Cognitive models of writing', *German as a Foreign Language*, 2–3, pp. 7–22.

Gerlach, M. and Altmann, E. G. (2013) 'Stochastic model for the vocabulary growth in natural languages', *Physical Review X*, 3(2), p. 021006. Available at: https://doi.org/10.1103/PhysRevX.3.021006.

Gobet, F., Lane, P. C. R., Croker, S., *et al.* (2001) 'Chunking mechanisms in human learning', *Trends in Cognitive Sciences*, 5(6), pp. 236–43. Available at: https://doi.org/10.1016/S1364-6613(00)01662-4.

Goldberg, A. E. (1995) *Constructions: A Construction Grammar Approach to Argument Structure*. Chicago, IL: University of Chicago Press.

Goldberg, A. E. (2003) 'Constructions: A new theoretical approach to language', *Trends in Cognitive Science*, 7(5), pp. 219–24.

Goldberg, A. E. (2006) *Constructions at Work: The Nature of Generalization in Language*. Oxford: Oxford University Press.

Goldberg, A. E. (2019) *Explain Me This: Creativity, Competition, and the Partial Productivity of Constructions*. Princeton, NJ: Princeton University Press.

Goodman, L. A. and Kruskal, W. H. (1954) 'Measures of association for cross classifications', *Journal of the American Statistical Association*, 49, pp. 732–64.

Grant, T. (2007) 'Quantifying evidence in forensic authorship analysis', *International Journal of Speech Language and the Law*, 14(1), pp. 1–25. Available at: https://doi.org/10.1558/ijsll.v14i1.1.

Grant, T. (2010) 'Txt 4n6: Idiolect free authorship analysis', in M. Coulthard (ed.) *Routledge Handbook of Forensic Linguistics*. London: Routledge, pp. 508–23.

Grant, T. (2022) *The Idea of Progress in Forensic Authorship Analysis*. Elements in Forensic Linguistics. Cambridge: Cambridge University Press. Available at: www.cambridge.org/core/elements/idea-of-progress-in-forensic-authorship-analysis/6A4F7668B4831CCD7DBF74DECA3EBA06.

Grant, T. and MacLeod, N. (2018) 'Resources and constraints in linguistic identity performance: A theory of authorship', *Language and Law / Linguagem e Direito*, 5(1), pp. 80–96.

Grant, T. and MacLeod, N. (2020) *Language and Online Identities: The Undercover Policing of Internet Sexual Crime*. Cambridge: Cambridge University Press.

Gries, S. T. (2013) '50-something years of work on collocations: What is or should be next', *International Journal of Corpus Linguistics*, 18(1), pp. 137–66. Available at: https://doi.org/10.1075/ijcl.18.1.09gri.

Grieve, J. (2007) 'Quantitative authorship attribution: An evaluation of techniques', *Literary and Linguistic Computing*, 22(3), pp. 251–70.

Grieve, J., Clarke, I., Chiang, E., *et al.* (2019) 'Attributing the Bixby Letter using n-gram tracing', *Digital Scholarship in the Humanities*, 34(3), pp. 493–512.

Halliday, M. A. K. and Matthiessen, C. M. I. M. (2004) *An Introduction to Functional Grammar*. London: Arnold.

Halvani, O., Graner, L., and Regev, R. (2020) 'Cross-domain authorship verification based on topic agnostic features', in L. Cappellato, C. Eickhoff, N. Ferro, and A. Névéol (eds.) *Working Notes of CLEF 2020: Conference and Labs of the Evaluation Forum*. Available at: https://ceur-ws.org/Vol-2696/.

Hasan, R. (1996) 'Ways of saying: ways of meaning', in C. Cloran, D. Butt, and G. Williams (eds.) *Ways of Saying, Ways of Meaning: Selected Papers of Ruqaiya Hasan*. London: Cassell, pp. 191–242.

Hasan, R. (2009a) 'On semantic variation', in J. Webster (ed.) *The Collected Works of Ruqaiya Hasan Vol. 2: Semantic Variation: Meaning in Society and in Sociolinguistics*. London: Equinox, pp. 41–72.

Hasan, R. (2009b) 'Wanted: A theory for integrated sociolinguistics', in J. Webster (ed.) *The Collected Works of Ruqaiya Hasan Vol. 2: Semantic Variation: Meaning in Society and in Sociolinguistics*. London: Equinox, pp. 5–40.

Hasson, U., Chen, J., and Honey, C. J. (2015) 'Hierarchical process memory: Memory as an integral component of information processing', *Trends in*

Cognitive Sciences, 19(6), pp. 304–313. Available at: https://doi.org/10.1016/j.tics.2015.04.006.

Hawkins, R. P. and Dotson, V. A. (1968) 'Reliability scores that delude: An Alice in Wonderland trip through the misleading characteristics of interobserver agreement scores in interval coding', in E. Ramp and G. Semb (eds.) *Behavior Analysis: Areas of Research and Application*. Englewood Cliffs, NJ: Prentice Hall.

Hayek, L.-A. C. (1994) 'Analysis of amphibian biodiversity data', in R. W. Heyer *et al.* (eds.) *Measuring and Monitoring Biological Diversity: Standard Methods for Amphibians*. Washington, DC: Smithsonian Books, pp. 207–70.

Heaps, H. S. (1978) *Information Retrieval: Computational and Theoretical Aspects*. Library and Information Science Series. New York: Academic Press.

Herdan, G. (1960) *Type-Token Mathematics*. Janua linguarum, Series maior, 4. 's-Gravenhage: Mouton.

Hilpert, M. (2014) *Construction Grammar and Its Application to English*. Edinburgh: Edinburgh University Press.

Hoey, M. (2005) *Lexical Priming: A New Theory of Words and Language*. London: Routledge.

Hoover, D. L. (2004) 'Testing Burrows's Delta', *Literary and Linguistic Computing*, 19(4), pp. 453–75.

Houvardas, J. and Stamatatos, E. (2006) 'N-gram feature selection for authorship identification', in J. Euzenat and J. Domingue (eds.) *Artificial Intelligence: Methodology, Systems, and Applications*. AIMSA 2006, Bulgaria. Berlin: Springer, pp. 77–86. Available at: https://doi.org/10.1007/11861461_10.

Hudson, R. (2010) *An Introduction to Word Grammar*. Cambridge: Cambridge University Press.

Hudson, R. A. (1996) *Sociolinguistics*. 2nd ed. Cambridge Textbooks in Linguistics. Cambridge: Cambridge University Press.

Hunston, S. and Francis, G. (2000) *Pattern Grammar: A Corpus-Driven Approach to the Lexical Grammar of English*. Edited by G. Francis. Studies in Corpus Linguistics, 4. Amsterdam: John Benjamins.

Ishihara, S. (2021a) 'Score-based likelihood ratios for linguistic text evidence with a bag-of-words model', *Forensic Science International*, 327, p. 110980. Available at: https://doi.org/10.1016/j.forsciint.2021.110980.

Ishihara, S. (2021b) 'The influence of background data size on the performance of a score-based likelihood ratio system: A case of forensic text comparison', in *Proceedings of the 18th Workshop of the Australasian Language*

Technology Association. ALTA, pp. 21–31. Available at: https://aclanthology .org/volumes/2020.alta-1/.

Jaccard, P. (1912) 'The distribution of the flora in the alpine zone', *New Phytologist*, 11(2), pp. 37–50. Available at: https://doi.org/10.1111/j.1469-8137.1912 .tb05611.x.

Jafariakinabad, F. and Hua, K. A. (2021) 'Unifying lexical, syntactic, and structural representations of written language for authorship attribution', *SN Computer Science*, 2(481), pp. 1–14. Available at: https://doi.org/ 10.1007/s42979-021-00911-2.

Jain, A. K., Ross, A., and Prabhakar, S. (2004) 'An introduction to biometric recognition', *IEEE Transactions on Circuits and Systems for Video Technology*, 14(1), pp. 4–20. Available at: https://doi.org/10.1109/TCSVT .2003.818349.

Jannidis, F., Pielström, S., Schöch, C., and Vitt., T. (2015) 'Improving Burrows' Delta: An empirical evaluation of text distance measures', in *Digital Humanities Conference 2015*. Sydney, Australia: Alliance of Digital Humanities Organizations.

Johnson, A. and Wright, D. (2014) 'Identifying idiolect in forensic authorship attribution: An n-gram textbite approach', *Language and Law/Linguagem e Direito*, 1(1), pp. 37–69.

Johnstone, B. (1996) *The Linguistic Individual: Self-Expression in Language and Linguistics*. Oxford: Oxford University Press.

Juola, P. (2008) 'Authorship attribution', *Foundations and Trends® in Information Retrieval*, 1(3), pp. 233–334. Available at: https://doi.org/ 10.1561/1500000005.

Juola, P. (2012) 'Large-scale experiments in authorship attribution', *English Studies*, 93(3), pp. 275–83.

Jurafsky, D. and Martin, J. H. (2009) *Speech and Language Processing: An Introduction to Natural Language Processing, Computational Linguistics, and Speech Recognition*. Upper Saddle River, NJ: Pearson/ Prentice Hall.

Keller, R. (1994) *On Language Change: The Invisible Hand in Language*. London: Taylor & Francis.

Kestemont, M. (2014) 'Function words in authorship attribution from black magic to theory?', in *Proceedings of the 3rd Workshop on Computational Linguistics for Literature (CLfL) @ EACL 2014*. Gothenburg, Sweden: Association for Computational Linguistics, pp. 59–66.

Kestemont, M., Stover, J., Koppel, M., Karsdorp, F., and Daelemans, W. (2016) 'Authenticating the writings of Julius Caesar', *Expert Systems With Applications*, 63, pp. 86–96. Available at: https://doi.org/10.1016/j.eswa.2016.06.029.

Kestemont, M., Manjavacas, E., Markov, I., *et al.* (2020) *Overview of the Cross-Domain Authorship Verification Task at PAN 2020*, Available at: https://pan.webis.de/downloads/publications/papers/kestemont_2020.pdf.

Kidd, E., Donnelly, S., and Christiansen, M. H. (2018) 'Individual differences in language acquisition and processing', *Trends in Cognitive Sciences*, 22(2), pp. 154–69. Available at: https://doi.org/10.1016/j.tics.2017.11.006.

Kidd, E., Bidgood, A., Donnelly, S., Durrant, S., Peter, M. S., and Rowland, C. F. (2020) 'Individual differences in first language acquisition and their theoretical implications', in C. F. Rowland, A. Theakston, B. Ambridge, and K. Twomey (eds.) *Current Perspectives on Child Language Acquisition: How children use their environment to learn.* Amsterdam: John Benjamins, pp. 189–219. Available at: https://doi.org/10.1075/tilar.27.09kid.

Koppel, M. and Schler, J. (2004) 'Authorship verification as a one-class classification problem', in *Proceedings of the 21th International Conference on Machine Learning*. Banff, Alberta, Canada: ACM, pp. 62–7.

Koppel, M. and Winter, Y. (2014) 'Determining if two documents are written by the same author', *Journal of the Association for Information Science and Technology*, 65(1), pp. 178–87.

Koppel, M., Schler, J., and Argamon, S. (2009) 'Computational methods in authorship attribution', *Journal of the American Society for Information Science and Technology*, 60(1), pp. 9–26.

Koppel, M., Schler, J., and Argamon, S. (2011) 'Authorship attribution in the wild', *Language Resources and Evaluation*, 45(1), pp. 83–94. Available at: https://doi.org/10.1007/s10579-009-9111-2.

Koppel, M., Schler, J., and Argamon, S. (2013) 'Authorship attribution: What's easy and what's hard?', *Journal of Law and Policy*, 21, pp. 317–31.

Kulczynski, S. (1927) 'Die Pflanzenassociationen der Pienenen', *Bulletin International de l'Academie Polonaise des Sciences et des Lettres. Classe des Sciences Mathematiques et Naturelles. Serie B. Sciences Naturelles*, Suppl. II(2), pp. 57–203.

Lakoff, G. (1990) 'The Invariance Hypothesis: Is abstract reason based on image-schemas?', *Cognitive Linguistics*, 1(1), pp. 39–74. Available at: https://doi.org/10.1515/cogl.1990.1.1.39.

Lancashire, I. (1997) 'Empirically determining Shakespeare's idiolect', *Shakespeare Studies*, 25, pp. 171–85.

Lancashire, I. (2010) *Forgetful Muses: Reading the Author in the Text*. Toronto: University of Toronto Press.

Langacker, R. W. (1987) *Foundations of Cognitive Grammar*. Stanford, CA: Stanford University Press.

Leeuwen, D. A. van (2015) *ROC: Compute Structures to Compute ROC and DET Plots and Metrics for 2-Class Classifiers*. R package. Available at: https://rdrr.io/github/davidavdav/ROC/.

Lewis, D. D., Yang, Y., Rose, T. G., and Li, F. (2004) 'RCV1: A new benchmark collection for text categorization research', *Journal of Machine Learning Research*, 5, pp. 361–97.

López-Monroy, A. P., Montes-y-Gómez, M., Villaseñor-Pineda, L., Carrasco-Ochoa, J. A., and Martínez-Trinidad, J. F. (2012) 'A new document author representation for authorship attribution', in *Mexican Conference on Pattern Recognition*. Berlin: Springer, pp. 283–92. Available at: https://doi.org/10.1007/978-3-642-31149-9_29.

Mccauley, S. M. and Christiansen, M. H. (2015) 'Individual differences in chunking ability predict on-line sentence processing', in D. C. Noelle, R. Dale, A. Warlaumont, *et al.* (eds.), *Proceedings of the 37th Annual Conference of the Cognitive Science Society*. Pasadena, CA: Cognitive Science Society, pp. 1553–8.

McMenamin, G. R. (2002) *Forensic Linguistics: Advances in Forensic Stylistics*. Boca Raton, FL: CRC Press.

Mikros, G. K. and Argiri, E. K. (2007) 'Investigating topic influence in authorship attribution', in B. Stein, M. Koppel, and E. Stamatatos (eds.), *Proceedings of the SIGIR 2007 International Workshop on Plagiarism Analysis, Authorship Identification, and Near-Duplicate Detection*, vol. 276. Amsterdam: CEUR-WS.org. Available at: http://ceur-ws.org/Vol-276.

Miller, G. A. (1956) 'The magical number seven, plus or minus two: Some limits on our capacity for processing information', *Psychological Review*, 63 (2), pp. 81–97.

Mollin, S. (2009) '"I entirely understand" is a Blairism: The methodology of identifying idiolectal collocations', *International Journal of Corpus Linguistics*, 14(3), pp. 367–92. Available at: https://doi.org/10.1075/ijcl.14.3.04mol.

Mosteller, F. and Wallace, D. L. (1963) 'Inference in an authorship problem', *Journal of the American Statistical Association*, pp. 275–309. Available at: https://doi.org/10.2307/2283270.

Mountford, M. D. (1962) 'An index of similarity and its applications to classificatory problems', in P.W. Murphy (ed.) *Progress in Soil Zoology*. London: Butterworths, pp. 43–50.

Murauer, B. and Specht, G. (2021) 'Developing a benchmark for reducing data bias in authorship attribution', in *Proceedings of the 2nd Workshop on Evaluation and Comparison of NLP Systems (Eval4NLP 2021)*. Association

for Computational Linguistics, pp. 179–88. Available at: https://aclanthology
.org/2021.eval4nlp-1.18.pdf.

Narayanan, A., Paskov, H., Gong, N. Z., *et al.* (2012) 'On the feasibility of internet-scale author identification', in *Security and Privacy (SP), 2012 IEEE Symposium on.* IEEE, pp. 300–14. Available at: https://ieeexplore.ieee.org/document/6234420.

Nini, A. (2018) 'An authorship analysis of the Jack the Ripper letters', *Digital Scholarship in the Humanities*, 33(3), pp. 621–36.

Nini, A. and Grant, T. (2013) 'Bridging the gap between stylistic and cognitive approaches to authorship analysis using Systemic Functional Linguistics and multidimensional analysis', *International Journal of Speech Language and the Law*, 20(2), pp. 173–202.

Nini, A., Cameron, M., and Murphy, C. (2021) 'Experimental evidence on the individuality of lexicogrammar', in *International Construction Grammar Conference 11 (ICCG11).* Antwerp: University of Antwerp. Available at: https://doi.org/10.5281/zenodo.5227222.

Oakes, M. P. (2014) *Literary Detective Work on the Computer.* Amsterdam: John Benjamins.

Ochiai, A. (1957) 'Zoogeographic studies on the soleoid fishes found in Japan and its neighboring regions', *Bulletin of the Japanese Society of Fisheries Science*, 22, pp. 526–30.

Pearson, K. and Heron, D. (1913) 'On theories of association', *Biometrika*, 9, pp. 159–315.

Petré, P. and Van de Velde, F. (2018) 'The real-time dynamics of the individual and the community in grammaticalization', *Language*, 94(4), pp. 867–901.

Pinker, S. (1994) *Language Instinct.* New York: William Morrow.

Plakias, S. and Stamatatos, E. (2008) 'Tensor space models for authorship identification', in J. Darzentas, G. A. Vouros, S. Vosinakis, and A. Arnellos (eds.) *Proceedings of the 5th Hellenic Conference on Artificial Intelligence (SETN'08).* Syros, Greece: LNCS, pp. 239–49.

Pokhriyal, N., Tayal, K., Nwogu, I., and Govindaraju, V. (2017) 'Cognitive-biometric recognition from language usage: A feasibility study', *IEEE Transactions on Information Forensics and Security*, 12(1), pp. 134–43. Available at: https://doi.org/10.1109/TIFS.2016.2604213.

Proisl, T., Evert, S., Jannidis, F., Schöch, C., Konle, L., and Pielström, S. (2018) 'Delta vs. n-gram tracing: Evaluating the robustness of authorship attribution methods', in *Proceedings of the Eleventh International Conference on Language Resources and Evaluation (LREC-2018).* Miyazaki, Japan: European Language Resources Association (ELRA), pp. 3309–14.

Renouf, A. and Sinclair, J. (1991) 'Collocational frameworks in English', in K. Aijmer and B. Altenherg (eds.) *English Corpus Linguistics: Studies in Honour of Jan Svartvik*. London: Longman, pp. 128–43.

Rogot, E. and Goldberg, I. D. (1966) 'A proposed index for measuring agreement in test-retest studies', *Journal of Chronic Disease*, 19, pp. 991–1006.

Russell, P. F. and Rao, T. R. (1940) 'On habitat and association of species of Anopheline larvae in South Eastern Madras', *Journal of the Malaria Institute of India*, 3, pp. 153–78.

Sapkota, U., Bethard, S., Montes-y-Gómez, M., and Solorio, T. (2015) 'Not all character n-grams are created equal: A study in authorship attribution', in *Human Language Technologies: The 2015 Annual Conference of the North American Chapter of the ACL*. Denver, CO: ACL, pp. 93–102.

Sari, Y., Vlachos, A., and Stevenson, M. (2017) 'Continuous N-gram representations for authorship attribution', in *Proceedings of the 15th Conference of the European Chapter of the Association for Computational Linguistics*, pp. 267–73. Available at: https://doi.org/10.18653/v1/e17-2043.

Schmid, H.-J. (2015) 'A blueprint of the Entrenchment-and-Conventionalization Model', *Yearbook of the German Cognitive Linguistics Association*, 3(1), pp. 3–25. Available at: https://doi.org/10.1515/gcla-2015-0002.

Schmid, H.-J. and Mantlik, A. (2015) 'Entrenchment in historical corpora? Reconstructing dead authors' minds from their usage profiles', *Anglia*, 133 (4), pp. 583–623. Available at: https://doi.org/10.1515/ang-2015-0056.

Schmid, H.-J., Würschinger, Q., Fischer, S., and Küchenhoff, H. (2021) 'That's cool: Computational sociolinguistic methods for investigating individual lexico-grammatical variation', *Frontiers in Artificial Intelligence*, 3, p. 89. Available at: https://doi.org/10.3389/frai.2020.547531.

Schmitt, N. (2004) *Formulaic Sequences: Acquisition, Processing, and Use*. Amsterdam : John Benjamins.

Seidman, S. (2013) 'Authorship verification using the impostors method', in P. Forner, R. Navigli, D. Tufis, and N. Ferro (eds.) *CLEF 2013 Evaluation Labs and Workshop – Working Notes Papers*. Valencia, Spain, pp. 23–6. Available at: https://ceur-ws.org/Vol-1179/.

Shannon, C. E. (1948) 'A mathematical theory of communication', *Bell System Technical Journal*, 27, pp. 379–423 & 623–56.

Simpson, G. G. (1943) 'Mammals and the nature of continents', *Amercian Journal of Science*, 241, pp. 1–31.

Sinclair, J. (1991) *Corpus, Concordance, Collocation*. Oxford: Oxford University Press.

Smet, H. De (2016) 'The root of ruthless: Individual variation as a window on mental representation', *International Journal of Corpus Linguistics*, 21(2), pp. 250–71. Available at: https://doi.org/10.1075/ijcl.21.2.05des.

Smith, P. W. H. and Aldridge, W. (2011) 'Improving authorship attribution: Optimizing Burrows' Delta method*', *Journal of Quantitative Linguistics*, 18 (1), pp. 63–88. Available at: https://doi.org/10.1080/09296174.2011.533591.

Sokal, R. R. and Michener, C. D. (1958) 'A statistical method for evaluating systematic relationships', *University of Kansas Science Bulletin*, 38, pp. 1409–38.

Sokal, R. R. and Sneath, P. H. A. (1963) *Principles of Numerical Taxonomy*. San Francisco, CA: W.H. Freeman.

Solan, L. M. and Tiersma, P. M. (2005) *Speaking of Crime: The Language of Criminal Justice*. Chicago, IL: University of Chicago Press.

Sorgenfrei, T. (1958) 'Molluscan assemblages from the marine middle Miocene of South Jutland and their environments', *Danmark Geologiske Undersøgelse. Serie 2*, 79, pp. 403–8.

Stamatatos, E. (2009) 'A survey of modern authorship attribution methods', *Journal of the American Society for Information Science and Technology*, 60 (3), pp. 538–56. Available at: https://doi.org/10.1002/asi.21001.

Stamatatos, E. (2013) 'On the robustness of authorship attribution based on character n-gram features', *Journal of Law and Policy*, 21(2), pp. 421–39.

Svartvik, J. (1968) *The Evans Statements: A Case for Forensic Linguistics*. Gothenburg: University of Gothenburg Press.

Todeschini, R., Consonni, V., Xiang, H., Holliday, J., Buscema, M., and Willett, P. (2012) 'Similarity coefficients for binary chemoinformatics data: Overview and extended comparison using simulated and real data sets', *Journal of Chemical Information and Modeling*, 52(11), pp. 2884–901. Available at: https://doi.org/10.1021/ci300261r.

Turell, M. T. (2010) 'The use of textual, grammatical and sociolinguistic evidence in forensic text comparison', *International Journal of Speech Language and the Law*, 17(2), pp. 211–50.

Turell, M. T. and Gavaldà, N. (2013) 'Towards an index of idiolectal similitude (or distance) in forensic authorship analysis', *Journal of Law and Policy*, 21, pp. 495–514.

Ullman, M. T. (2004) 'Contributions of memory circuits to language: the declarative/procedural model', *Cognition*, 92(1–2), pp. 231–70. Available at: https://doi.org/10.1016/j.cognition.2003.10.008.

Ullman, M. T. (2013) 'The role of declarative and procedural memory in disorders of language', *Linguistic Variation*, 13(2), pp. 133–54. Available at: https://doi.org/10.1075/lv.13.2.01ull.

Vetchinnikova, S. (2017) 'On the relationship between the cognitive and the communal: A complex systems perspective', in M. Filppula, J. Klemola, A. Mauranen, and S. Vetchinnikova (eds.) *Changing English*. Berlin: De Gruyter, pp. 277–310. Available at: https://doi.org/10.1515/9783110429 657-015.

Warrens, M. J. (2008) 'Similarity coefficients for binary data'. Unpublished thesis, Leiden University.

Wible, D. and Tsao, N.-L. (2010) 'StringNet as a computational resource for discovering and investigating linguistic constructions', in *Proceedings of the NAACL HLT Workshop on Extracting and Using Constructions in Computational Linguistics*. Los Angeles, California, USA, pp. 25–31. Available at: https://aclanthology.org/W10-0804/.

Wray, A. (2008) *Formulaic Language Pushing the Boundaries*. Oxford: Oxford University Press.

Wright, D. (2013) 'Stylistic variation within genre conventions in the Enron email corpus: Developing a text-sensitive methodology for authorship research', *International Journal of Speech Language and the Law*, 20(1), pp. 45–75.

Wright, D. (2017) 'Using word n-grams to identify authors and idiolects: A corpus approach to a forensic linguistic problem', *International Journal of Corpus Linguistics*, 22(2), pp. 212–41. Available at: https://doi.org/ 10.1075/ijcl.22.2.03wri.

Yule, G. U. (1900) 'On the association of attributes in statistics', *Philosophical Transactions of the Royal Society*, 75, pp. 257–319.

Yule, G. U. (1912) 'On the methods of measuring association between two attributes', *Journal of the Royal Statistical Society*, 75, pp. 579–642.

Acknowledgments

Many colleagues, students, and friends helped me make this work much better than it would have otherwise been thanks to their comments, thoughts, and suggestions and for the engaging and stimulating conversations that emerged as a result. A big thank you to Colin Bannard, Dagmar Divjak, David Wright, Ewa Dąbrowska, Henri Kauhanen, Jack Grieve, Jonathan Dunn, Marcelo Montemurro, Michael Cameron, Miranda Watson, Ricardo Bermúdez-Otero, Richard Zimmermann, and Vera Hohaus.

A very special thanks to Stephanie Evert and Shunichi Ishihara, whose work had a major impact on mine and whose feedback and input was crucial.

I would also like to thank the anonymous reviewers and the series editors, in particular Tammy Gales, who followed this project closely with patient and warm support.

Cambridge Elements ≡

Forensic Linguistics

Tim Grant

Aston University

Tim Grant is Professor of Forensic Linguistics, Director of the Aston Institute for Forensic Linguistics, and past president of the International Association of Forensic Linguists. His recent publications have focussed on online sexual abuse conversations including *Language and Online Identities: The Undercover Policing of Internet Sexual Crime* (with Nicci MacLeod, Cambridge, 2020).

Tim is one of the world's most experienced forensic linguistic practitioners and his case work has involved the analysis of abusive and threatening communications in many different contexts including investigations into sexual assault, stalking, murder, and terrorism. He also makes regular media contributions including presenting police appeals such as for the BBC *Crimewatch* programme.

Tammy Gales

Hofstra University

Tammy Gales is an Associate Professor of Linguistics and the Director of Research at the Institute for Forensic Linguistics, Threat Assessment, and Strategic Analysis at Hofstra University, New York. She has served on the Executive Committee for the International Association of Forensic Linguists (IAFL), is on the editorial board for the peer-reviewed journals *Applied Corpus Linguistics* and *Language and Law / Linguagem e Direito*, and is a member of the advisory board for the BYU Law and Corpus Linguistics group. Her research interests cross the boundaries of forensic linguistics and language and the law, with a primary focus on threatening communications. She has trained law enforcement agents from agencies across Canada and the United States and has applied her work to both criminal and civil cases.

About the Series

Elements in Forensic Linguistics provides high-quality accessible writing, bringing cutting-edge forensic linguistics to students and researchers as well as to practitioners in law enforcement and law. Elements in the series range from descriptive linguistics work, documenting a full range of legal and forensic texts and contexts; empirical findings and methodological developments to enhance research, investigative advice, and evidence for courts; and explorations into the theoretical and ethical foundations of research and practice in forensic linguistics.

Cambridge Elements ≡

Forensic Linguistics

Elements in the Series

The Idea of Progress in Forensic Authorship Analysis
Tim Grant

Forensic Linguistics in the Philippines: Origins, Developments, and Directions
Marilu Rañosa-Madrunio and Isabel Pefianco Martin

The Language of Fake News
Jack Grieve and Helena Woodfield

A Theory of Linguistic Individuality for Authorship Analysis
Andrea Nini

A full series listing is available at: www.cambridge.org/EIFL

Printed in the United States
by Baker & Taylor Publisher Services